PATTERNS OF PARTNERSHIP

MARRIAGE: PATTERNS OF PARTNERSHIP

Beulah Wood

with
STUDY GUIDE

OM
publishing

First published in 1998 by OM Publishing

04 03 02 01 00 99 98 7 6 5 4 3 2 1

OM Publishing is an imprint of Paternoster Publishing,
P.O. Box 300, Carlisle, Cumbria, CA3 0QS, U.K.
http://www.paternoster-publishing.com

British Library Cataloguing in Publication Data
A catalogue record for this book is available from the British Library.

ISBN 1-85078-316-0

Cover design by Forum, Newcastle upon Tyne
Typeset by WestKey Ltd, Falmouth, Cornwall
Printed in Great Britain by Mackays of Chatham PLC, Kent

Dedication

In memory of my husband Brian Wood,
with whom I learnt the intimacy of
shared decisions.

Contents

Foreword

This book is neither a manual on how to achieve the perfect marriage, nor a resource for counselling troubled marriages. Rather, it is an exploration of the way husbands and wives in the Bible related to each other and what God expected of them, especially in relation to decision-making within their marriages.

Stories from our own life and times illustrate the struggles, decisions and solutions of real people today and show how shared decisions can work out in practice.

There are some surprising conclusions too, to make us look more carefully at the teachings we may legitimately draw from the Bible.

Beulah Wood
Bangalore, India,
March 1998

1

Spotlight on a Decision

Here is the problem

One Monday afternoon I turned the little green Honda motor cycle between the whitewashed gateposts of the school, leaning slightly to the right to keep the balance for my pillion, Dorothy. I switched the handlebars to the left and wound the throttle to a roar as we ascended the steep clay and gravel drive between the trees and up to the big pitch where my husband Brian, was releasing the First Eleven boys to go up to their dormitories after cricket practice.

Oh, dear. He had little Kaaren on his shoulders. That must have been a nuisance for him while he was coaching. Taking Dorothy on up to the top of the drive, I parked the bike outside the staff room and hurried back to Brian. The practice had run late, I could tell. I'd expected him to finish in time to collect Kaaren from a friend on the staff and look after her from 5.30p.m., but the time was now 5.40p.m.

Brian lifted Kaaren over his head, threw her, grinning, in the air as he always did, caught her, and balanced her back on the ground on her sturdy little legs. We laughed to each other as she ran, arms outstretched, to meet me. What a little ball of energy we had. Brian slung her back aloft his shoulders again as we climbed the stone steps. Soon we sauntered along the bank above the botanical gardens to our flat that had been converted from nineteenth-century stables.

Living on this wooded hillside at 7,500 feet in the South Indian town of Ootacamund, we taught at Lushington School with its 120 sons of missionaries and business people and a smaller number of Indian schoolboys.

I started talking about the fading light of the varying greens in the gardens below, but Brian had something on his mind.

'Do you think you could give up going to Emerald Heights on Mondays?' he asked. 'It's annoying to have to stop cricket in time to collect Kaaren. She was brought down to me, and then kept talking to me while I was trying to finish the practice.'

My mind flicked back rapidly to the messages I'd received at home and in church. I'd been told as long as I could remember that wives should obey their husbands. When we were planning our wedding, Brian asked if I was going to promise to obey and I said, 'Of course'. I knew one could not be a good Christian wife without that. Now I was being asked to put it into practice. He wasn't thinking about it that way, of course, but that's how it appeared to me.

Emerald Heights was a college for young women where Dorothy and I had just started a study group to encourage young Indian Christian women in their understanding of the Bible and the Christian life. It was the kind of thing I loved to do. I'd gained experience at leading Bible studies in my own undergraduate days and it was a treat to leave the school compound and relate to young women instead of boys, and to thinking young people instead of minding my baby.

That year the women's college was one of only two spots in the week when I could use my training as a classroom teacher. The other was a Sunday class when I went with another friend to a small English medium school for young Indian boys. During the week I minded the clothes of a dormitory of boys. I also worked several afternoons at summarising a theological classic, *Calvin's Institutes,* into easy English ready for translation into Tamil, and taught beginner piano pupils. But the largest portion of my time went into happily caring for my little girl.

Though I wished I could teach a Bible class, it wasn't considered appropriate for a woman to teach a high school level boys' Bible class, and it wouldn't have worked because Brian was already teaching a class, and someone had to look after Kaaren. So, trained teacher as I was, the only class teaching I did that year was the two Scripture classes, one hour each, on Sunday and Monday.

In contrast, Brian taught all day, supervised 'prep' once a week, taught music theory on Saturday morning, coached sport two or three afternoons after school, taught a Bible class on Sunday, and trained the choir most lunch-times as well. He loved relating to boys, cared about them, drew great cooperation from them, and I was proud to see him make such a significant contribution. After all, we were in India for Brian to support the work of missionaries by enabling them to stay because their sons were being adequately educated. And I was there to support Brian, and help a little in the school when this could fit around his needs and those of our little daughter. Most of the time I was quite happy with this. It was what I expected.

So now Brian's question. It took me less than half a minute to reply, 'Yes. Sure. If you find it a pressure that I'm away late afternoon both Sunday and Monday, I'll stop going on Monday. My job is to enable you to do your task here, not to put extra stress on you.'

We unlocked the door, got a bath ready for Kaaren, and set the table for the evening meal.

I decided to talk to Dorothy that evening about our decision. She'd have to go alone and would have to take a taxi. It had been a lot easier when we went together with me driving the small motor bike. But she'd have to accept that. She didn't drive herself.

As far as I could see all the staff knew that wives did as their husbands wished. It was part of our background as evangelical Christians. My mind turned to the young women I'd started to get to know in the Emerald Heights class – a few well-grounded in Bible teaching, some with just the beginnings of faith. We used to enjoy learning to understand each other, them as young able

Indian undergraduates, me as a little older Westerner resident in their town.

I felt a pang as I thought about not meeting with them again, and losing the class, but in another way I felt good about the decision. I'd read something similar in the book that was a model on missionary endeavour for us reaching adulthood in the 1960s, Elizabeth Elliott's *Shadow of the Almighty*. Elizabeth's husband Jim had asked her to obey him in a specific issue and she had obeyed. It seemed I was in good company.

Brian did not say much about the suggestion I had accepted. Perhaps it was not a big deal with him. I treated it as a natural decision myself, and did not think about it very long. I was merely following through a previously accepted personal attitude.

Looking back now, I wonder why I let it pass so rapidly. I did not explain to Brian how much I enjoyed the two hours in the week when I actually had a class in front of me, when I could teach, use my training, endeavour to pass on Christian truths to young folk in our city, and when I was not limited to the company of a toddler. I didn't tell him I liked the young women and wanted to keep meeting with them to encourage them to grow in Christian faith. He may have seen it differently if he had realised that if only he made a point of finishing the cricket on schedule he would have enabled me to continue to be part of this Christian work.

What kind of person was I that I did not even care to explain my wishes to my husband? I did not even pray about it – ask God to show me what I should do. Was my briefly considered action so obviously correct that it needed no second opinion, or even a prayer? Does the Bible say, or does it not say, that a wife must obey her husband?

And where is a decision made anyway? I may think my husband made the decision that I cease to teach the class, but when I look harder, I realise I decided as much as he. I decided to follow along with his wishes. That's something women need to look at more closely. We cannot off-load decisions as easily as we may wish.

But doesn't the Bible say a husband as the head of the house is to make decisions for the family? And isn't a husband to be a covering to shield his wife from making wrong decisions?

Does it matter?

Kaaren is 26 now, and I have pondered many more times who makes the decisions in the home, and who does what work. We taught for eight years in that school amid the waves of decisions that come and go in family life. We twice took several months back in New Zealand. Then we felt God led us to Nepal where Brian was principal of another boys' boarding school. As we approached our thirteenth wedding anniversary, he lost his life in a fall high up in the Himalayan mountains.

For 15 years as a widow bringing up four daughters, the ways in which husbands and wives relate, or believe God wishes them to relate, have often set us thinking. We have tried to understand marriages we are in contact with because it affects the way I raise my girls, and now their own thinking about the kind of relationships they want.

We hear preaching, read books and meet assumptions about the biblical pattern for marriages using passages that seem to explicitly discuss relationships in 1 Corinthians 11, Ephesians 5 and 1 Peter 3. These we certainly must study, and a number of writers have explored these passages in recent years.

For this book I have taken a different tack. I have analysed some of the marriages described in the Old and New Testaments to find the patterns of how decisions were made, which patterns God approved of, and who God treated as accountable for decisions, actions and their consequences. Some Bible marriages were disasters. Some were wonderfully successful. Picking out what made the difference was a voyage of discovery.

Then I looked out for stories to tell from life in the twentieth century, from my own marriage, and from couples I met who think hard about their decisions together. Our over-riding question is: Does God expect a married woman to be responsible for her actions, along with the rewards and punishments? Or does God plan that her husband make the decisions and take the responsibility for her?

2

A Question of Accountability

Who is responsible?

When I knew him, Jonathan was a hard working young missionary in India. He kept tightly scheduled hours writing Bible studies for local Christian leaders, and preaching, often with translation, for scattered groups of believers on Sundays. He was not very fluent in the language yet, so he still took lessons, practised with his teacher, and studied carefully through his sermon preparation to get the right words and phrases.

The work was challenging and he loved it. This was what he had trained for at Bible school in Britain two years before. He had become engaged to Julie, who came from a neighbouring church in his city, while he was at Bible school. Taking the advice of his seniors he went ahead for 18 months to start adjusting to Indian life and culture before flying home to be married and to bring Julie back to Motipur village. (Names and circumstances have been altered to preserve anonymity.)

They were an uncomplicated couple to start with. Jonathan felt God had called him to missionary work and his church leaders commended him to go to India. He would lead the family and make the decisions for them as a couple and in their Christian work. Julie believed, like her husband, that God's call on her life was to be Jonathan's wife.

So Julie arrived in India. The welcome the first evening from the village church was especially for her, but she did not realise the people's efforts. As she and Jonathan walked from the mission compound across a small field to the whitewashed church building, she trod in a cow pat. Not what she was used to – coming from the city. It upset her, offended her that she had to put up with such a revolting thing. But Jonathan treated it lightly – just part of life here, he explained. Julie still felt offended about it weeks later.

During the evening people said hello and then she felt left out of the conversation because of the language barrier. She didn't put herself out to talk to those who did have some English.

That evening became fairly typical of Julie in Motipur. She took some language lessons but she did not learn very quickly. She was there to be Jonathan's wife. That was all that was required – be a wife and mother. That was a woman's role. That was the pattern for Christian women, they and their church believed.

She was a mother in a while too. Baby Nick was a healthy little boy. Now it was difficult for Julie to travel with Jonathan when he went to village churches to preach. She still could not talk to the people, and Jonathan was busy. She stayed home and wished he'd stay home more during the week too. He spent so much time with the senior missionary, working on the Bible study courses they were writing, relating to the people in the little churches. He was so devoted to his work. Why did he not spend more time with her when she was on her own at home with Nick day after day? There was so little to do. She could make a big deal out of walking over with Nick to spend time with the senior missionary's wife for a while each day, just for something to do. Sometimes she'd stay two hours. She made Jonathan promise to do something with her every Saturday night. They played board games.

And then there was the worry about Nick. What if he became ill with one of the infections that were so easy to catch? All the Westerners drank only boiled water, but Nick slurped his bath water. Julie boiled the bath water in the morning and allowed it to cool so that when she bathed him before dinner it would be the right temperature. Then when he was learning to walk they got sand for him to play in, but he ate some of the sand. That could make him sick too, Julie feared. She boiled the sand. She was so afraid of all the germs. And there was so little else to think about but Nick, and the meals for Jonathan.

Julie was increasingly unhappy – depressed in fact. She could not stand Motipur. She whinged at Jonathan every time he returned to the house. Why didn't he spend more time with her, she would ask. Why couldn't they move to the city? She wore Jonathan down. He realised she was unhappy. Something had to change and he persuaded his seniors there was work they could do in the city. They moved there. But Julie was still depressed. Jonathan helped with church work, but Julie saw only negatives. Her depression continued. It ruined everything for them. In the end Jonathan had to give up his missionary work and take Julie home to England.

So what went wrong for this couple? Most mission societies have known for decades that both members of a couple need to experience a sense of call to missionary work. One person cannot receive the guidance for another. If a person merely follows along, the pressures will soon show them up. Missionary work requires joint decision making by a couple. The problem arose for Julie and Jonathan because Julie had never decided for herself that God had called her to India. She was trying to live her life on Jonathan's guidance. And the weakness was not picked up because they belonged to a mission group that occasionally used very inexperienced decision makers.

Using a mission example shows up the need for joint decisions in an obvious way. But any marriage can work better with joint decisions when the decisions affect both the husband and wife: whether one person will do shift work, whether one is a full-time Christian worker in their own country, whether the family will move to a different town.

Some women don't bother having an opinion

When churches, books and radio preachers teach repeatedly, with their understanding of the Bible, that the husband is the head of the house, earning the money and making all major decisions, couples try to live that out, even if in practice a couple may find it does not sit comfortably with them. What if the wife is better at looking after the finances? What if the husband is ill and can't work, or out of work, or has an alcohol problem? What if the wife is a teacher and better understands the children's needs and can make the important decisions on their schooling? Or perhaps she is a musician and speaker and can lead the worship in her church and the position requires her to also be an elder although her husband is not?

Women can placidly acquiesce to the belief that men should make decisions until they let life happen round them and take no initiatives. It happens in this day and age. I see Christian women who have never developed their talents. I see secular women who have let society's acceptance of men as leaders rob them of even wanting to decide about their own lives.

I have a younger friend, call her Barbara, who tells how when she and her husband were trying to save money they lived for a while with another young married couple so they could share the rent and food costs. The other man took a fancy to Barbara. She recalls the day he and her husband sat in the kitchen and discussed who would have her. The other man won and she went off with him to Australia.

I'm horrified by the story not only because of Barbara and her husband's lack of commitment to their marriage, and because there didn't seem to even be any major problems between them at the time, but by the fact that Barbara had so little self esteem that she did not think it was important to have an opinion herself as to which man would carry her off! And this occurred in Western society, not a country where there are arranged marriages and where women may be viewed as goods to make decisions about. More than this, Barbara was brought up in a secular home where she had not received the frequent pulpit teaching I sat under about obeying the men in one's life.

In the 1980s researchers wanted more than anecdotal evidence on how much say women had in major decisions. They carried out a survey on family decision making of all the women in Wellington, the capital of New Zealand, with the surname Smith. The idea was that the surname used by all social and economic levels in society would be representative of the whole New Zealand society. They found 80% of the women allowed major decisions affecting them to be made by the men in their lives – their husbands, fathers, sons, boyfriends. They were letting life happen round them and allowing themselves to be irresponsible.

Sometimes couples act more equally than they realise

My husband Brian and I never analysed how we made decisions. I thought he should be or was the head of the house. I was brought up with the teaching that the men are God's ordained leaders. I thought one could not be a good Christian without obeying one's husband if there was a dispute. That's why I said I'd stop teaching the Scripture class on Monday afternoons when we worked at the school in South India.

But that is one of the few examples I can think of. Much more often we decided jointly on things that were important and affected us both. I will tell some stories about that later, and some when we did not agree.

I think now that deciding together must be the way many Christian couples operate, even when they suppose the husband should make the decisions. If a husband truly loves his wife, he does not ride roughshod over her wishes anyway. When husbands act as total despots and wives act as passive doormats, the chances are high for depression, break-down or violence. Domestic violence figures of many countries make that obvious.

Are women responsible?

As a university student, and later teacher, missionary, journalist and writer, networking with many evangelical charismatic and pentecostal Christians and missions, I have met hundreds who define themselves as Christians who take seriously the authority of the whole Bible for life and faith. My friends always teach that every human being is accountable to God for their actions. That's my kind of theology too.

But there's a conflict here if the same groups teach that men make the decisions and lead while the women follow. Women could not be held responsible for their actions if they must obey husbands. If women must have decisions made for them, they can never be rewarded for the right decision, nor punished for the wrong one.

Adults often make decisions for children, because they see them as not mature enough to be fully accountable for their actions. If women may act only on the decisions made for them by husbands, they are being treated as no more than children.

But does a law court treat women as not accountable for their actions, so that they can claim the decision was taken by a husband? The answer may be *Yes* in a Muslim country. But it is certainly *No* in Western legal systems. They expect a woman to be accountable for her actions.

I talked to my solicitor about this to make sure I got the correct story. The system in New Zealand law, which is based on both common law and written law from Britain, used to be that matrimonial property was vested in the husband. Under that law a married woman was permitted to 'pledge her husband's credit', meaning that in making a purchase at a shop she could sign that her husband would pay the bill. She acted as his agent in managing the household.

Changes to this concept were codified in law in New Zealand in 1976 with the Matrimonial Property Act. The preamble to this said it was

> An act to reform the law of matrimonial property to recognise the equal contribution of husband and wife to the marriage partnership . . . and to affirm the legal capacity of married women. The rights, privileges, powers, capacities, duties and liabilities of a married woman shall . . . be the same in all aspects as those of a married man

whether she is acting in a personal, official, representative or fiduciary capacity.

A woman has the same responsibilities as a man. If they run a business together, they are both responsible to declare their income to the taxation department, even if he tells her not to. Or in a dispute with a neighbour, if they both own the property, they may both be summoned for a court appearance.

In a criminal case a wife would be tried in her own right, even if her husband told her to sell the stolen goods. She would probably be an accessory after the crime, or a co-defendant if she was part of the crime.

This would be true in most countries of the world. A few years ago as part of my work as Communications Manager for an aid agency I went to Tanzania where we visited a village of the Masai tribe which extends across the borders of Tanzania and Kenya. Our informants told us how in the eyes of these people a woman is always a child – never fully responsible. These Tanzanian friends thought, correctly, that I as a Western woman would not approve of this view.

But my thoughts went along the lines, 'Funny thing that. These people are at least honest in stating openly that they think a woman is legally no more than a child. But I have repeatedly heard and read the implication that women must have decisions made for them from preachers and Christian writers who still teach that a woman must obey her husband.'

People hide from the inconsistency of their thinking. They teach that every individual is responsible to God for their own actions, and will be rewarded or punished for their actions, and then tell a wife to obey her husband. How can she be responsible for her actions?

The odd thing is that there are still thousands of Christians who have never thought through the inconsistency of their argument that a husband is always the final authority in a marriage.

For contrast, here's one of the most stark examples in all the Bible of God requiring a woman to be accountable for her actions rather than the husband taking sole responsibility for a family decision. It comes from Acts 5.

Ananias and Sapphira

In the fledgling church in Jerusalem people were selling their possessions and goods and distributing the proceeds to all who had needs, spending much of the day together at the temple. Whenever they ate food they felt glad and generous, feeling good about everyone and praising God. One Jewish couple, church members called Ananias and Sapphira, thought this was great and decided to join in. They also sold some property and took the money to the church, with one difference. They agreed to keep for themselves some of the sale price and not tell anyone, just revealing as the sale value the figure they intended to give to the church's pool of funds.

It looked simple. They would be supported by the pooled system, but they would have a nest egg to draw on as well. Ananias went to make his very generous donation and placed it at the feet of the apostles – it certainly was generous. The trouble was the lie he told when he gave a lower figure as the amount the purchaser had paid. The Holy Spirit told the apostle Peter something was amiss, and he remonstrated.

'Ananias, why has Satan filled your heart to lie to the Holy Spirit and to keep back part of the proceeds of the land? While it remained unsold, did it not remain your own? And after it was sold, were not the proceeds at you disposal? How is it that you have contrived this deed in your heart? You did not lie to us but to God.'

Ananias promptly fell down and died. Struck dead by God. Heart attack? We do not know. The terrified church members rushed around so fast organising a burial they didn't even tell his wife, which in most societies would be a major omission.

But the significant thing for our understanding of accountability within marriage happened when Sapphira hurried down to the meeting place three hours later, probably wondering what had delayed her husband. When Peter asked her how much they sold the land for she gave the same fiddled figure her husband had offered. Peter was extremely hard on her.

'How is it that you have agreed together to put the Spirit of the Lord to the test? Look, the feet of those who have buried your husband are at the door, and they will carry you out.'

She promptly fell down dead too. Whether again from shock or an act of God the result was the same – punishment. Now here is my question. If Sapphira was only obeying her husband as a good Christian wife should obey the only accepted decision maker in the human partnership, why did God strike her dead? Was that fair, if she was only doing what she was told?

In fact when we look carefully at the Acts 5 story, we find she was fully part of the decision they made. Verses 1 and 2 say 'With the consent of his wife Sapphira,' and 'With his wife's knowledge he kept back some of the proceeds.'

God recognised her part in the decision and held her accountable for her actions. If God treated Sapphira as totally under the control of her husband, he could not punish her because it would not be her right to go against his wishes.

Recognised for rewards or punishments

We find over and over in the Bible that God treats both women and men as responsible for their actions. He has to. If he plans to save men or women depending on their response to his offer of salvation, and punish them depending on their failure to accept his offer, they must each be responsible for their own actions, not having decisions made for them by another human being.

And if a husband or a church leader could hand down decisions for a woman or a wife in such a way that she must obey him without being accountable, he would stand between a woman and God – a priest or mediator. But the New Testament says, 'There is one mediator between God and humankind, Christ Jesus.' 1 Timothy 2:5

We have to accept that when people are part of God's family and try, or do not try hard enough, to follow Jesus' pattern for living, they are still each responsible for their own actions. But even in this closing decade of the twentieth century I meet Christian couples who try so hard to follow the teaching about the husband being the head of the home, that the wife will leave a decision affecting herself or both of them, or the whole family, to the husband. And scores of Christian preachers, marriage seminars and books tell them the same thing.

Perhaps they think that when Christian wives reach heaven and stand before the judgment seat of Christ, and Christ asks them how they used their talents, or why they did not teach a Sunday school class or make friends with their neighbours in order to tell the good news of the Kingdom of God, they plan to answer, 'Don't ask me, God. Ask my husband. He made the decisions in our household. Isn't that what you told us to do?' And she will attempt to stand behind her husband so he can answer for her.

But God may say to them, 'That is not what I meant. Go and look at what is written in the New Testament.'

Let me list some of the verses that tell us we are answerable to God for ourselves, no mention ever of decision making by husbands that is binding on wives. These passages are some of the most basic to all the Bible's teaching of reward and punishment for individual human beings.

- God, through Jesus Christ, will judge the secret thoughts of all. Romans 2:16
- We will all stand before the judgment seat of God. Romans 14:10
- In the presence of God and of Christ Jesus, who is the judge of the living and the dead. 2 Timothy 4:1
- From now on there is reserved for me the crown of righteousness, which the Lord, the righteous judge, will give me on that day, and not only to me but also to all who have longed for his appearing. 2 Timothy 4:8
- But they will have to give an account to him who stands ready to judge the living and the dead. 1 Peter 4:5
- Then I saw a great white throne and the one who sat on it . . . And I saw the dead, great and small, standing before

> the throne, and books were opened. Also another book was opened, the book of life. And the dead were judged according to their works, as recorded in the books . . . and all were judged according to what they had done. Revelation 20:11–13

The inescapable conclusion is that God expected all men and all women to be responsible for their actions. Bible believing people cannot have it both ways. If we say humans must give account to God for their actions, we cannot say at the same time that one group, wives, take orders from husbands.

And what happens to the wives who do try to be fully obedient? Some become so passive that they are unable to speak up when they believe a husband's decision is completely wrong. They are left obeying a husband more than God. And I do not think that is what we who rely on the Bible mean to teach.

3

Philosophy in a Nepalese Tea Shop

God loves girls as much as boys

The scene is the middle hills of Nepal near the large town of Pokhara. Free from his school principal's duties on Saturday, Brian and I walk up the valley through the grain fields with daughters Kaaren, Bronwyn, Adrienne and Rosalind. We pause beside a Nepalese tea shop strategically placed beside the walking path and near the fields. We order glasses of the hot sugary stewed tea, and a young woman pours it with her black ladle. She's looking at our family.

'Ek, dui, tin, char,' she counts. 'Are they all girls or is that one a boy?' She points with her chin to 10 year old Kaaren dressed in shorts and not wearing the apparently essential glass bangles.

'That's my jethi chhori, my oldest daughter,' I respond. 'They're all girls.'

'All girls?' the young woman echoes, glancing to see whether I'm pregnant again, whether I'm making the required attempt to bear a son. It's terribly important here. We have met the question so often and have our answer ready.

'We love girls just as much as boys. And we have a God who loves girls as much as boys.'

The young woman looks at me puzzled. She thinks I've got my Nepali words muddled because I am saying two things that do not add up in her thinking. A God who loves, and who loves girls as much as boys. Not possible. Not in the view of a culture that sees Gods as capricious and unpredictable towards all people. A culture that sees women and girls as a burden requiring a dowry and useless to the family economy because they will go to a husband's home.

Girls start working for their household carrying firewood and pots of water from age 6 and 7, so young their friends at the water tap have to help them get the load to shoulder height before they plod down the stony path with a burden that strains their far-from-mature backs. Many are kept from school so they can carry out the farmstead tasks. By the time they reach fifteen they are years into their working life, while fifteen year old boys will have received the chance to go to school and still have leisure to play marbles as the girls walk past with loads on their backs. Yet with all their work, girls are not valued. Everyone wants sons.

Brian used to ask the people, 'Why are you so anxious to have a son?' A son is essential to carry out the funeral rites to get parents into Nirvana. Besides that, a son is reckoned to support his parents in their old age while a daughter will, they believe, contribute only to the wealth of her husband's family.

Repeatedly that year in Nepal this conversation opener gave us the chance to talk about a God who loves, and loves girls as much as boys.

I look at women in church

The next year I was back in New Zealand, and without Brian since he had died on the mountain slopes above the tea shops we used to visit. My mourning took months of working through, and as I came out the other side, attempting to settle myself and my four daughters in a community and church in my home country, I found I faced an unexpected complication. Something did not seem right in the Western Christian scene about the value of women. We had said God loves girls as much as boys, but gradually I realised it did not look like that in church. It affected me and my daughters even though there was no father in the home, because it coloured how others viewed us in our church and among our acquaintances.

I saw marriages where women were told they had the same status as men, but were treated with less status. Marriages in which men expected to take all the major decisions or have the last word as if the wife was a lesser being with lesser mental powers. Marriages where women lost confidence and lost the ability to take initiatives because they were always expected to follow their husbands. I saw girls growing up less challenged than boys because it seemed they would never have to take as much responsibility in the home or the church.

I was not surprised that women were less able to lead. They often did not get the training or the practical experience. This is how it may happen.

In the year when my seventeen-year-old acquaintance won her high school's prizes for both public speaking and debating, her church youth group organised two youth services on Sunday evenings at the church. The first time they asked a young man her age to give the five minute sermon. I surmised that the leaders must see something in him that they wanted to encourage and that was fair enough. But when they asked him to speak the second time, ignoring the gifts of the girl, it seemed an unfair discrimination, though probably quite unconscious. My young friend and her youth group friends were not even aware of the injustice that a talented girl was twice overlooked in favour of a guy. In the same year a group of young people taking sermon classes received the chance to deliver a sermon in church. They were all young men.

If people say the reason women receive less leadership opportunities in a church is because they are less skilled and less experienced at the up-front tasks, I agree. But the fault lies with the church rather than the lack of women. Churches rarely give young women the encouragement and practice they give young men. And similarly within a marriage, if a woman is less qualified to take an equal share of decision making, it is often because she has received both less encouragement and less experience at making major decisions, and has grown up thinking that is not required of women. But the additional problem is that even when she is experienced and able, she receives less recognition than a man.

That question of status?

A leader of my former church told me I was wrong to say the church gives women less status than men. 'God's plan is for men and women to have equal status and different function,' he said. 'This is what it means when Paul wrote in Galatians 3:28, "There is no longer Jew or Greek, there is no longer slave or free, there is no longer male and female; for all of you are one in Christ Jesus."'

I could comment for comparison that I haven't noticed the Christian Church in the last few decades saying there is one function for Jews and another for non-Jews, nor that there is one function in the church for economically advantaged and another for disadvantaged, even though that may happen in practice at times. While women's and men's biological functions are different, need this require all their social, mental, work-related and family functions also to be different? It would be difficult to extract from the Bible a necessary connection of all other areas of life to biological differences.

I saw in my church, leaders claiming that while women were equal in status with men, their function was to act unequally because they were not expected to hold responsibility to make decisions except in the areas allotted them. So what do we mean by status? In most societies people show in three possible ways that the status of someone is high – by giving them formal positions or symbols of importance; by letting them make the decisions and rules and obeying them; or by paying them highly.

In Western society we give status to a person by using titles such as 'Your Honour' to a judge, by a chain of office for a mayor, or by a place at the top table at a formal dinner. The Maori and Pacific Island cultures around us in Auckland show status by giving the important people such as the elders the first food at a feast, or having them speak first at a formal function.

The same is true in India even within the family, where often women must give food first to the parents-in-law and the husband and eat the leftovers later themselves, because they hold lower status. And in India and Nepal I've seen civic leaders accord high status to visiting dignitaries by putting archways across the road and by providing an escort of gleaming motor bikes or a fleet of shiny cars. Does our church sub-culture give the symbols of status to both men and women?

The second way of recognising status is allowing those with status to make the rules and by obeying them. If we do not wish to accept their status we may be forced to. Decisions made by school teachers, company managers, employers, and police must generally be obeyed. On a smaller scale folk of many cultures give status to their old people by obeying their wishes. Does your church or mine give the same number of positions where the decisions and rules are made to women and men?

Thirdly, in any business, institution or agency it's a universal language readily understood that the people with the highest status receive the highest salary. In view of this, we could ask concerning our churches and denominations, do women receive the same level of salary as men? Or are there as many salaries for women? Or do they even receive a salary? All of us in churches should work for the kingdom of God unpaid some of each week, but readers may like to check whether in their church the proportions of men's and women's paid and voluntary work are the same.

If in our church life women are not visibly receiving the same status as men, we as church members have fallen far behind our theory. No wonder I became uneasy about my statement as a missionary among Hindu people that God loves girls as much as boys. I still think my statement is true. The problem is with our practice.

In the Beginning

We have seen equality briefly mentioned in Galatians. We need now to look further through the Bible to obtain a fuller picture, with Genesis and the creation of humans as a starting point.

Genesis 1:27 says 'So God created humankind in his image, in the image of God he created them; male and female he created them.' The unique thing about God making humans was that they were made like their Creator. This is significant for our discussion since it applies to both male and female humans. If women and men are both made in God's image, we must conclude they are each as much like God as the other, and it is not acceptable to say one is more like God or must dominate over the other. And if people argue that a man is a better representative of God, in the family or in the church, because he is more like God, they merely look with human minds.

God is not male or female, with the tangible bodily organs of a human. God is above gender. The convention of calling God 'He' is just that – a convenience for our language. Like a number of other languages, English has no personal pronouns other than 'he' or 'she'. We have no neuter which can apply to either a man or a woman. The nearest we have is 'it', which is impersonal, and we prefer not to refer to God Almighty as 'It.' All the same, when we're honest, our theology tells us we must recognise that God is neither a 'He' nor a 'She'.

For the same reason, addressing God as Father is a convenience, a very long-standing and traditional convenience going right back to one occurrence in the Old Testament in the prophecy of Isaiah. The famous Christmas-time passage in Isaiah 9:6, speaks of 'Everlasting Father, Prince of Peace'. But the description was not common till New Testament times.

Jesus spoke of God as Father, and that must have been natural to a Jew in a society which gave higher status to fathers than to mothers. It would have sounded very odd to them, to address God as Mother, or even as Eternal Parent. So Jesus used the metaphor of God as Father, as he used dozens of other metaphors like Light, Door, Water, Vine-grower, Comforter. It was useful picture language.

In the nature of things, God is not the physical father, by a sexual act, of the people who call their God Father. That is metaphor. The Creator creates in ways that do not require gender, neither as a father nor as a mother. But we humans often still speak of God as Father because we need the picture language. Jesus understood that, and used the picture language too.

In summary then, the lesson we can take from Genesis 1:21 is that neither a man nor a woman is any more like God than the other.

Adam and Eve

Partners helping each other

We move on to Genesis 2:18 where we find the Lord God said, 'It is not good that the man should be alone; I will make him a helper as his partner.' Thank the Lord for that. Life would be dull indeed if we were all men or all women. But the word 'helper' is often misunderstood here. It can be taken to indicate lower status in the way an employee helps an employer who remains in the higher position. But that is not the way the word is used most often in the Bible.

The word translated here as helper refers 15 times to the Holy Spirit of God who stands beside a human as an advisor or consultant – not a lower position, more one of greater knowledge and experience whose advice will be followed. The word can also mean a partner when the two partners are equal in a partnership. For me that abolishes any hesitations about 'helper'. It allows us to see such a position as no less than the person who is helped, and hence, if a woman is called the helper of man in Genesis 2, she may as readily be his advisor or consultant or equal partner as his assistant taking orders.

Why did Eve give in to temptation?

As we move to Genesis 3, we come to the one story that illustrates something of how Adam and Eve related to each other and to God. We need to look at how they made decisions and how much God expected them each to be accountable for their actions.

When the serpent held a long conversation with Eve about whether they had permission to eat the fruit, and the advantages or otherwise of eating it, it was such persuasive stuff that she gave in and passed some to Adam who ate too. There was verbal pressure but no force. They each ate of their own free will. But somehow, suddenly, their relationship was changed. They both had been naked and unashamed. Now they each felt there was something they wanted to hide. They made clothes. Next they hid from their only friend, their Creator. They agreed about both these moves, but then they blamed each other. 'It's the woman's fault,' accused Adam, or even perhaps, 'Your fault, God, for giving her to me.' And Eve in turn blamed the serpent.

But could any blame be slipped from the shoulders so easily? Unless there is physical force, allowing oneself to be persuaded is a decision a person makes. He or she cannot lay blame on another. Adam decided to accept and eat the fruit, and Eve decided to eat and give some to Adam. Each acted as a free agent.

In Genesis 2:18,24,25 Adam and Eve were partners in pleasure. In Genesis 3:7–8 they were partners in guilt. God punished them both. There is no suggestion that Eve could take the blame for both because she sinned first, nor that Adam should be punished more because he was the head of the household and therefore more responsible.

The punishments for Eve were pain in childbirth, and the fact that her husband imposed his domination over her. A peculiar interpretation came out of that punishment last century. It was taken to mean that if a woman had a difficult labour, nobody should attempt to alleviate her pain. It was merely God's will. In fact doctors who gave pain relief to women in labour could be taken to court in some Christian countries. This century it is okay to work against that curse for women, but many are reluctant still to work against the other curse of male domination.

We do not hesitate to work against the consequences of Adam's punishment either. Humans endeavour to enrich the ground against the curse of unproductiveness and weeds, and develop machinery to avoid the labour intensive cropping methods of hoe or ox-plough, though still three quarters of the farming men and women of the world use them.

One interpretation of this chapter is that Eve sinned because she handled the discussion with the serpent by herself without asking her husband's advice. When I came upon this view after Brian had died I grew nearly speechless with indignation.

'How,' I wanted to know, 'am I supposed to resist temptation without a husband then? It would be impossible and I would be forever falling into sin, if a woman can only resist sin with the help of a husband. And what about all the single women? And how, may I ask, am I supposed to raise my four daughters, if neither they nor I can resist sin, until I can deliver them safely into the hands of some unsuspecting husband who will protect them from trouble for ever after?'

The view simply does not wear with the facts of how people's lives are. God does not arrange for every woman to have a husband. That is not even statistically possible since, in all but four countries of the world where women are very badly neglected and discriminated against, there are more women than men. I can only conclude that God requires me and my daughters to resist temptation now, not wait for some knight in shining armour to rescue me from the weakness of female frailty.

Besides this, our theology says Jesus did away with the evils caused by the curse. Not completely, I guess, since humans still contend with pain in childbirth, thorns and thistles and hard physical work. The law of Moses is also seen as part of the curse, and Galatians 3:13,14 says, 'Christ redeemed us from the curse of the law by becoming a curse for us . . . in order that in Christ

Jesus the blessing of Abraham might come to the Gentiles, so that we might receive the promise of the Spirit through faith.'

On this basis one could argue that as we seek to live under the rules of the kingdom that Jesus is establishing, we should no longer live by the rules of a past age in which husbands ruled wives. Instead it would be time to live by the new rules of the blessings brought by Jesus Christ and the power of the Holy Spirit.

The conclusion we can draw from the story of Adam and Eve and their surrender to temptation is that they were each free to act, they each made a decision (whether they blamed someone else or not), and the Lord God expected each to take the consequences of their own decision.

None of us can hide behind another human being. The only place we can hide is at the foot of the cross of the divine Son of God, who alone can relieve us of the punishment for our actions. But that is a truth which only became apparent later than Adam and Eve in the revelation of God's plan for people.

4

On the Road

Learning from each other

The long passenger train rolls to a stop as it clanks through the back of the brick and once cream-washed plaster buildings of Delhi. It is 5.00p.m. and we have been on the railroad over 72 hours. Now we've lined up Brian with his big backpack, bags of empty drinking water bottles, Kaaren and Bronwyn each with a little backpack, and me with a child pack for 2-year old Adrienne and another bag in my hand. We're ready for the onslaught. The red shirted coolies will storm the carriage when it stops, but the Wood family will push their own way out and avoid the hassle of arguments over what to pay a coolie.

Now we're out in the hurly burly of the Indian railway station. 'Karfee, karfee, garum dudh, chai,' the vendors yell with their coffee, hot milk or tea, while coolies jog past with 40 kilogram tin trunks balanced on their heads. Friend Mike (one of the leaders of Interserve – the mission society we would later join) meets us and guides us to a taxi and home to his place where we meet Betty.

'Welcome to our place,' she greets us in their upstairs flat. 'You must be tired after your three days on trains with the children. Where are you heading for after your weekend with us?'

'We're on our way further north,' Brian replies. 'We're spending Christmas with the Birch family.'

'Sounds an interesting trip. Well, do relax for your time with us. We'll enjoy putting you up. Stay with us on the way back if you wish, too. When will that be?'

'After three weeks. About the second week of January,' Brian replies.

'Three weeks,' echoes Betty. 'That's a very long time to stay for a holiday. Are you sure it's all right with them?'

'Perfectly sure,' Brian and I respond. 'We know the Birches well.'

'But you need to think about it,' Mike adds. 'They'll have their work to do. We've seen it with other people. Most hosts would find it too much to have a family stay that long.'

'Oh, it really is okay,' I explain. 'The Birches are good friends of ours.'

On reflecting

Looking back, I realise we hardly thought about Mike and Betty's caution. We were so sure we were right. I should have remembered the many times Brian had invited himself to stay with friends. He used to do it frequently when he was single. He kept doing it when there were two of us and then three, four, five as our children arrived, but he was sure it was not a problem. Earlier I felt awkward asking to stay with people, thinking we would be extra work for the woman of the family, but I got over my inhibitions so well that I joined Brian. I suggested Christmas with the Birches (not their real name). I wish I had kept to my earlier intuition.

We took the long train trip north a few nights later, were met by Russell Birch who had generously come the long bus trip to bring us to their rented mission house perched on a roadside in a little mountain town. Russell and Mary and the children welcomed us and gave us the run of the downstairs stone-walled basement of their narrow village house. They introduced us to goat curry in the evenings and chappatis with honey and cream for breakfast. We celebrated Christmas with them and the small group of hill men and women who made up the little church in the Muslim population. We travelled with the Birches – another long winter-chilly mountain bus trip through beautiful alpine snow fields. We viewed the scenery – mountains, rivers and lakes and saw exquisite handcrafts worked in the long cold winter weather.

Several days remained when we returned to the Birches' village. Their children had only the holidays to be with their parents as a complete family and here we, teachers from their boarding school, were taking up family time. We found little to do in the village and we had to work at entertaining our children. Mary became ill and spent three days in bed. We were not regretful when it was time to go. Brian and I would have done better to heed the thoughts of Mike and Betty, I realised later. I think we stayed too long.

So how had we come to make that decision? I remember it too well. Though I previously felt sensitive about not taking advantage of friends' hospitality, I had let myself be over-ruled by Brian's enthusiasm for visiting till I took a page from his book and even took the initiative in seeking an invitation, forgetting to be aware of others' feelings. They probably would have said if we asked how long to stay, 'Yes, come for Christmas week.'

I would have made a better decision if I had held to my own earlier perceptions and got Brian to understand my hesitations, instead of moving to his position and so considerably inconveniencing another family.

Hospitality at Christmas again

I tried to learn that lesson of not inconveniencing hosts by staying too long, or staying when there were too many people. It was one we faced frequently when we travelled, trying to manage on very slim finances.

The next time the issue stands out in my mind occurred four years later when we were on leave in New Zealand and due to return to Nepal early in January, and again it was a matter of where to spend Christmas.

We looked forward to a full Wood family reunion that year. Brian's brother Derek and wife Gillian and two daughters would visit from Australia, and with his other brother and family in Auckland we would celebrate with Brian's mother and sister, Jenny. Derek and family would stay with Mother and Jenny in their moderate three bedroom house. I knew, as women know, that we six could not also stay with Mother. That would be too much worry, too much noise for an older lady, too many people for the house. But Brian did not agree. He dreamed of the fun of the children all waking up to Christmas presents in their grandmother's house.

Brian had commented to me just a month before that if I told him something was impossible, it made him determined to do it. So I did not tell him we totally could not stay with his mother. He was under pressure: speaking at meetings; doing building alterations; conducting choir practices; facing the looming departure; along with the strain of being the principal of a school with all the cross-currents of modern education in an ancient culture.

The pressure point decision occurred in November when my kind-hearted mother-in-law and Jenny were visiting us where we were staying temporarily in my home town, Putaruru, to be near my family. That Sunday afternoon Brian asked Mother if we could come to stay at Christmas. I knew she was so generous and loved her eldest son so much that she probably would not refuse him, even if it was more than she could manage. I rushed to the bedroom and prayed she would say No.

Moments later Brian came jubilantly to tell me it was all right. We could stay with his mother. I felt God had failed me. I went into hysterics. I had never done that before. I could have stopped myself, but I did not bother. What could I do if Brian would not listen to my view? But I gave up my self control, and that is no way to reason out a problem. At that stage, even though we did not always practise it, we still adhered to the theory that Brian was the final decision maker for the family.

Well, Brian took my worry seriously after that. The end of the story was that we did not stay with Mother, much to her secret relief. We enjoyed a few very happy nights with friends Hugh and Di and still spent the days of laughter and music of family reunion with the wider Wood family.

Now I have to analyse why Brian and I got into such a mess over that decision. I may have been right in realising we could not stay with Mother, but we were not talking it through. Brian could have discussed it better with me if he had not taken the attitude that he was right and opposition would only make him more adamant. And I could have discussed if I had not clammed up, or if we had already had a way of dealing with differences by talking them out. We did not have a system, probably because we didn't often disagree. But to have one person saying he would never accept 'Can't', and the other saying nothing, is not a recipe for good decisions. (With stories like this, you might think Brian and I had a stormy marriage. But believe me, we got it right a good many other times!)

The point of telling these two stories is that they show the difficulties we fell into when one person allowed intuitions to be over-ridden by the other, and when a couple believe that one person has the right to make a decision without reference to the other.

The Bible marriage to examine in this chapter also concerns a travelling couple and hospitality, and decisions made by one member of a couple without enough discussion.

Abraham and Sarah

Abraham and Sarah hide their relationship

Twice in the account of Abraham and Sarah, Genesis 12:10-20 and 20:1-8, the pair moved near to new Egyptain neighbours, and then King Abimelech. Both groups allowed them to stay. But Abraham was afraid for his safety. He was afraid the Egyptians, seeing his beautiful wife, would kill him in order to take her. So, with his request dressed carefully as a matter of life and death, which it may not have been for all he really knew, he told her, 'Say you are my sister.' In fact she was Abraham's half-sister.

The ruse worked only too well. Pharaoh's officials saw the beautiful woman and talked about her to their boss, who, sure enough, brought her into his household as a wife, probably one of several. And to get on to good terms with his brother-in-law, Pharaoh gave Abraham an abundant supply of sheep, oxen, donkeys, camels and slaves. Economically Abraham did well because of his trick.

But God, who did not agree with the plan, sent plagues on Pharaoh's household till he or his advisors realised the problem was that Sarah was already married. Not surprisingly, Pharaoh criticised Abraham severely for his lies.

'Why did you not tell me she was your wife? Why did you say, 'She is my sister' so that I took her for my wife? Now then, here is your wife, take her, and be gone.' And Pharaoh ordered his men to see Abraham on his way, out of the country, with his wife and all that he had.

But Abraham and Sarah were slow learners, it seems. They did the same thing all over again, this time in the Negeb, the semi-desert south of the Dead Sea. When Abraham said Sarah was his sister, King Abimelech took her, and again God had to intervene, this time with a dream for Abimelech, to rescue her from him and from Abraham's lies and cowardice.

Again a heathen king reprimanded Abraham for his deception, and it was all so unnecessary. God had not departed from Abraham. God even got him to pray for Abimelech and his barren wife and female slaves so that they bore children. It could have been so much more straightforward either to not go into the king's territory or to tell the truth and pray to Jehovah God for protection for both Sarah and Abraham.

When we analyse these situation we find one person made the decision, to selfishly save his own skin, with no thought of the distress and trauma suffered by his wife in entering the harems of two different eastern rulers. Abraham gained by it. Sarah lost. You could say Abraham used emotional blackmail.

One question we ask from our twentieth century perception is, 'Did Sarah have any options?' Could she have said, 'No, I won't tell or live this lie'?

There could have been serious consequences if she had not complied with Abraham's wish. If a husband threw out a wife there were few ways for a woman to survive because women could not own property, or work for wages, and Sarah was hundreds of miles from her own people. She would have to beg or be a slave or a concubine anyway.

But wait a minute. Before that ultimate step, Sarah surely had the option of talking. There is no indication that she attempted to talk Abraham out of his decision. Perhaps she was at fault in a measure too. Perhaps she gave Abraham too much power in the family. The power had surely gone to his head.

Sarah and Abraham want a son

The Jehovah God they worshipped, three times promised Abraham and Sarah a son. Genesis 12:2, 13:16, 15:1-6. They waited for decades. They needed a son. Besides, their ancient culture placed a heavy burden on a woman, or a man, that they were failures in life if they had no child. As with many Asian cultures today which place very high value on having children, the blame for lack of a child was often placed on the woman.

Sarah probably felt the social stigma, and certainly felt she was failing both God and Abraham. Desperately, she decided to do something about it. But she did not discuss it. She made the same mistake Abraham had earlier fallen into – making family decisions and then pushing the other into accepting, without enough talking over the question.

Genesis 16:1-6 tells how Sarah decided to have a surrogate child through giving to Abraham her Egyptian slave girl, Hagar. She does not appear to have asked Hagar or Abraham their feelings. Possibly Hagar knew she would lose her job if she did not comply, or perhaps she felt honoured to have sexual relations with the boss. And who can guess what Abraham thought. He had already shown such great faith believing that God would give him a son of his own to found a nation that 'the Lord reckoned it to him as righteousness'. In Romans 4 the apostle builds a whole doctrine on Abraham's faith in God even before the fulfilment of the promise of a son to himself and his wife.

It looks as if Sarah's action shifted Abraham from his great faith. Perhaps at this point she had taken too much power for herself. She certainly damaged their family life irretrievably.

Here we must stop to look at how a couple makes such decisions. Sarah took the initiative. Abraham complied. But in fact Abraham also made a decision. He decided to go along with Sarah's wishes without thinking it through for himself, or talking over with her the implications for themselves, their family, or God's promise that they two would have a son. They did not even pray about it.

Worse was to come. When Hagar did become pregnant, Sarah turned on Abraham, blaming him for the pregnancy and the fact that Hagar became uppity because she had succeeded where Sarah failed.

Worse yet. Abraham tried to shrug off any responsibility, though it was his child, by telling Sarah she could do what she liked as Hagar was in her power. Which she did, and treated her harshly. They were both guilty of inhumanity in using and abusing Hagar. They treated her as a thing, not a person. When Hagar ran away, God had to appear to her and guide her back to safety and the opportunity of herself becoming the mother of a nation.

The moral to these stories about Abraham and Sarah must surely be, husbands and wives should discuss decisions and make them together, asking God to guide. That's mutuality. Disaster followed when either Sarah or Abraham made decisions and pushed the other into compliance without enough considering or talking or praying.

But Abraham was the first of the patriarchs in the Bible, and patriarch means 'dominant father of the family'. We still use the word to describe a father-headed family. It's certainly interesting to realise he was not so totally dominant that he was never persuaded by his wife. Centuries of later teaching about father-headed families has taken father domination much further – even in New Testament times.

Abraham the Patriarch – How far did this go?

In view of Abraham's despicable behaviour in letting Sarah be pushed into the harem of a heathen king, the apostle Peter makes some startling statements.

In 1 Peter 3:1,5,6 we find these words: 'Wives, in the same way, accept the authority of your husbands . . . It was in this way long ago that the holy women who hoped in God used to adorn themselves by accepting the authority of their husbands. Thus Sarah obeyed Abraham and called him lord. You have become her daughters as long as you do what is good and never let fears alarm you.'

I felt horrified when I read that, remembering the story of how Abraham let Sarah risk sexual relations with another man, to save his own skin. Why should a woman accept that as a model of happy family life?

But the statement is softened by three things. The paragraph of verses 1-7 is probably addressed to the one member of a couple who is a Christian when the other partner is not. Such a wife, Peter advises, should try hard to fit the wishes of her non-believing husband, and such a husband should '. . . in the same way, show consideration for your wives in your life together, paying honour to the woman as the weaker sex, since they too are also heirs of the gracious gift of life – so that nothing may hinder your prayers.' (verse 7)

Looked at as instructions for either men or women, the advice is not so one-sided. A husband paying honour to a wife may lead to a very high level of consideration. It requires both women and men to watch out for the interests of their partner.

Then, verse 8, addressed to all the church members, instructs all to be considerate of everyone's needs in a way that would be impossible if a husband was indeed expected to be a dominating ruler of the house. 'Finally, all of you, have unity of spirit, sympathy, love for one another, a tender heart, and a humble mind.'

And the third softening of the statement about obeying a husband as much as Sarah did, comes when I realise that Sarah did, as we have seen above, take decisions in her own hands at times. The request to these Christian women to work in with their husband's wishes as much as Sarah did with Abraham's, was not as one-sided as it first appeared. Sarah and Abraham both made decisions.

God tells Abraham to obey Sarah

Then I noticed yet another story of Abraham and Sarah where, believe it or not, God told Abraham to take orders from Sarah.

Genesis 21:8-12 tells how on the day that the child Isaac, whom Sarah eventually bore to Abraham, was weaned, probably at age three or four, his mother saw Hagar's son Ishmael playing with him and told Abraham to throw out Hagar and her son so that Ishmael would not inherit any of Abraham's property along with Isaac. Abraham was terribly upset because Ishmael was his son. We do not know how God got the message through to Abraham, but it said, 'Do not be distressed because of the boy and because of your slave woman; whatever Sarah says to you, do as she tells you.'

That must have shocked a head-of-the-family patriarch. It would come as a shock to some of the Christian men in the twentieth century who claim they must rule their families in the way the patriarchs did. It could still shock some of the Christians who teach roles in family life that would have the husband / father always lay down the law for the rest of the family.

And that teaching is still being promoted, I noticed again last weekend at a camp for church women. The bookstall (and I must say the organisers were cross about this) contained among about 30 titles, 17 different books on marriage. For one thing my friends and I did not think there would be 17 different books on marriage at the men's camp the following month. Writers of Christian books, and selectors of books for women, often think it is alone the woman's task to hold a marriage together.

But on top of this, when I assessed the 17 titles on whether they taught mutuality of decision making or domination by the husband, only four taught mutuality. Five did not make clear the need for agreement, but talked more generally of communication skills, which is useful but inadequate if the reader does not learn that decisions must be made together. But eight books, published in Britain, United States of America and New Zealand, taught the domination of the wife by the husband.

Some surprising things show up about Abraham and Sarah, but the lesson looks clear. When Abraham made a decision without talking it over with Sarah, and without praying for God to guide, he made a mess. And Sarah brought trouble on herself if she acquiesced instead of talking it through till they reached agreement. In the same way when Sarah made a decision without talking with Abraham, and without praying for God to guide, she made a mess. And Abraham had also brought problems on himself by acquiescing instead of talking or praying.

Perhaps that is the biggest thing we can take from this whole book. A husband and wife need to decide things together – mutual decision making. If they do not, they can expect trouble.

5

How Could a Person Decide for Another Adult?

Joe and Helen

I have told some stories from Brian's and my marriage, and I want to tell about some other couples. Reading about other marriages will give us more to compare with, and keep us grappling with how marriage can work out for a Christian couple in our own times.

I asked Joe and Helen Cullen (not their real names) to help me illustrate this chapter because their experience as missionaries made them think very hard about the way they ran their marriage.

'I think I'm basically a caring sort of guy,' Joe says. 'When we were married, I took on board the responsibility to care for Helen. I wanted to be a godly man, so I believed, as I had been taught that God expected me to be responsible for decisions for my wife and family for their physical and spiritual life.

'The trouble was, at the back of my mind I didn't know how I'd do it. I had enough weaknesses of my own. How could I, a sinner, even if God was at work in me, decide what should happen for another adult human? Even after my year of Bible training I was wrestling with these principles I'd been told were biblical. Niggling underneath my belief that I was responsible for Helen's spiritual growth, I couldn't face the question, "What right have I to say how Helen should be? She's a child of God in her own right." But still I believed I should make decisions for us both.'

Helen felt the inner tension too, but she could not put it into words even to herself, let alone say it out loud. She could not even tell Joe.

'When we were married, I didn't want to say "obey", but I didn't dare leave it out,' she recalls. 'My parents would have thought that dishonoured God. I conformed because I wasn't strong enough to upset other people. I conformed for years. When I trained as a nurse, I hated the way the men doctors acted as if they were always right and the women nurses bowed and scraped unquestioningly. But I was only one nurse. I couldn't buck the system. It was there in our culture.'

'You see men's self-interest in leisure activities, not just work,' Joe adds. 'A guy likes to have a girl looking good in a bikini on a beach while he's out surfing – just for his image. And at the weekend married men seem to have full right to go out all day "with the boys" to watch sport and go to the sports club or pub and leave the wife to look after the children. It starts young, even among Christians. I've watched the young men play indoor soccer or basketball and the girls sit on the sideline and then make the supper. The whole evening is geared to the men.'

'As I grew up everyone thought the needs of boys and men were more important, and I didn't dare say anything,' Helen elaborates. 'For years I had to be someone I was not. Once early in our marriage we went to a Christian counsellor. He told Joe he was responsible for my well-being, to make me into a holy vessel. If I was a rebellious wife I was not walking with the Lord and that was Joe's responsibility. If that was true, I could sit down and put my feet up. And in my thinking now, that's a horror story. We even sat in church while a preacher told us an unmarried woman is under her father's control even if she's fifty.'

'I can criticise this position now,' Joe comments, 'but at first I bought into it. I couldn't see the faults because my whole background pushed in the old directions. In my head I know that these days Helen may have work to do and I may have to take a turn at cooking, but emotionally it's still a struggle. A friend told me, "If you let Helen have opinions of her own and do things like taking a part-time job, you're letting her wear the pants in your marriage." I can ignore that now. But I'm still learning to ignore the thoughts in me that say the prescription for how it is to be a man is that I can come home and find my wife has my dinner ready. My friend even said I shouldn't delay an important decision until we both agree, when there is a deadline. But I wouldn't want to push something through against Helen's wishes. Whether we let our names go on this story is a good example. One said, 'Yes, no problem', but the other said, 'No, not sure.' So we'll have to dialogue some more and decide together.'

Life in the mission society

Joe and Helen clashed no more than most others when they were first married. They do not think they were different from their Christian friends. But going overseas as missionaries made them realise they assumed things without realising. The mission had a task for Joe, and Helen kept busy with the children as they came along, and polished her skills at homemaking and hostessing. That was all she wanted for a while.

'I grew up thinking children and women should be seen and not heard,' she says. 'I had nothing much to say and thought my opinions useless and my skills worth little. I had a very low opinion of myself. That was also probably because I thought men and their work more important. But while we were there I grew and changed. I started to work part-time in mission tasks I was interested in. But then I felt criticised if I voiced an opinion. I thought some things could be improved but the mission structure didn't give wives a chance to say anything, only a chance to offer hospitality.'

'Then I took a study course, and started growing mentally. I realised I had some good ideas. I voiced them in class and people agreed. "Wow," I thought. "I've got some grey matter after all." I often sat and talked with an able middle-aged woman who said, "That's such a neat thought, Helen. You should write it down." Her reaction boosted my view of who I was. I stopped being afraid of my own opinions. I began thinking for myself.'

But then Helen started to comment about things in the mission that could be done better. Others thought she was critical or uncooperative. And Joe got the blame for not keeping his wife in order.

Did Helen have a right to speak?

'I felt frustrated with Helen,' Joe says. 'She wasn't becoming the person I wanted her to be – a demure Christian woman with an air of submissive spirituality. I wanted her to look right, say the right things, not have too many opinions – like other missionary couples who appeared to be successful.

'We felt more and more ill at ease with ourselves. We realised the roles we'd been wearing of "head of the family" and "submissive wife" were like masks to protect us from our inconsistencies, and from other people. And now the masks didn't fit any more. And Helen had taken hers off anyway.'

Joe didn't know which way to turn – support his wife, or support the men with whom he had to work every day. His loyalties were divided. Their marriage was a struggle. For years he believed, despite his nagging doubt, that he should be the head of the family. It had the ring of rightness. It was from the word of God, written in black and white as far as he could see. Not to be the head would undermine his manhood. Not to comply would bring a heavy guilt-trip of disobeying God.

People said Helen could make or break Joe's ministry. If he did not succeed, it would be Helen's fault because she was not being the kind of wife a man in his position needed.

'I felt like the meat in the sandwich,' Joe exclaims. 'Here I had Helen's opinions pushing me on one side and the mission people's expectation pressuring me on the other.'

Then Helen saw a major problem in the mission. Someone had to do something, and she said so. Joe agreed with her. Now he felt properly caught.

'Helen criticised my colleagues,' he explains. 'I'd have felt a whole lot more comfortable if Helen hadn't spoken out, if she had submitted. More tension. I hated having to choose between my wife and the mission. We clashed. And we clashed with them.'

'One thing helped keep me sane. I noticed that Ephesians 5:21 said, "Be subject to one another out of reverence for Christ." That meant mutual submission, me to Helen as much as Helen to me. Although for the sake of public peace I'd have liked Helen to 'submit', I couldn't ask it. We sat on a crisis. At times I felt like walking away from the mission to side with Helen. At times Helen could have walked away from both me and the mission.

'We'd been married 15 years when we took our third leave at home in New Zealand. We knew we had to go for help, to sort out our relation to each other, to our children and to the mission. We could not spend the rest of our life in such conflict. We booked with a counsellor.'

A new decision

'If I hadn't already felt discontented with the "male head" scenario, things wouldn't have changed so rapidly, but it was just what we needed,' Joe warms to the story. 'When the counsellor explained that the Greek word "head" does not necessarily mean authority, lights went on for me. In my thinking I stacked together the Bible passages saying each person is accountable for their actions with nobody deciding for another adult. I weighed against them the belief in male domination, telling another person what to do. I saw the theory of male leadership had to go.

'We rapidly made a new decision – we'd opt for mutual leadership in the home. In many ways we were already acting that way by then, going against roles of the past. Now we realised we were not disobeying the Bible. From then on the tension slipped away. We trusted each other more and shared more. I supported Helen in her views. I think now that we'll be learning for a long while yet. It's a pilgrimage. But if you think you've got it right, just because you're a man, you are less able to relate to your wife. Nobody should act in a way that says, "I have the edge, I am right, I'll teach you how to be like me," to another human being. And yet that's what you do if you believe that a man is always right.'

While the change in Joe's thinking wiped out much of the tension from him, Helen made changes too. When they returned to their missionary work, she stopped trying to get her sense of achievement through Joe or through the mission which didn't have a task for her. She concluded she did not like nursing. Her mother chose that career for her. She was good at empathising with people, but she would develop other strengths too. A little angrily she decided to do her own thing. While retraining by studying, she volunteered only for mission tasks she liked.

Imperceptibly at first, the tension of her relationship with the mission decreased. It was still there, and it still hurt fiercely at times, but it worried her and Joe less. They knew where they stood together in support of each other. And when later an important appointment came up, leading one section of the mission, it was offered to Joe and he could accept it without compromising Helen's ability to be true to herself.

Back in New Zealand the pilgrimage continues, they say. They feel they've worked out a style of support for each other that does not rely on one being confined to the private world and the other to the public world. Helen may not fulfill the unwritten expectation of a Christian leader's wife by doing the afternoon teas and waiting on guests, smiling, smartly dressed in the background. With her study and part-time job, Helen has commitments of her own.

'We teach seminars together, and I support Joe by talking with him about situations and difficulties. We're great friends,' Helen explains.

Joe reiterates. 'The support I like from Helen is for her to be my best friend. She's my confidante. I listen for her perspective.

I share everything with her. She challenges me if she feels I'm going in a direction that may not be appropriate. And I need that. My children challenge me now too. And I love it, because they speak to me directly rather than behind my back. We look at who each person is in the family horizontally, respecting each other as people, rather than vertically with father, then mother, then teenagers.'

'Sometimes I'm low and Joe pulls me up,' Helen fills in. 'Another time he may be at a weak point when I feel strong. Or one of the teenagers will write me an encouraging note when I feel down, or our 16-year-old will say, "Mum, you need a hug." Or indeed the 17-year-old may say to Joe, "Dad, my brother thinks you let him down in that area," and Joe will realise he's right and do something about it.'

Some people manipulate

Joe and Helen feel that among their church acquaintances, their attempt to live an equal marriage puts them in a minority. Seeing how some other couples act makes them squirm these days. They laugh about the old adage, 'He's the head and she's the neck' that people use to make the point that a woman has her own methods of getting her way.

'That just means she manipulates,' Helen laughs. 'Women can't get what they want if husbands never listen, so some become underhand. They say women nag. Often they do. And they use tone of voice, or become angry, or unresponsive, or cold to get their way. Or they withhold sexual favours, or don't allow a husband to touch them, or they act, "I'll make him pay." It's all because they can't discuss.'

A friend told Joe he should 'take a firmer hand' with Helen. 'I think I've worked out how his marriage is now,' Joe ponders. 'It too is manipulative. If his wife does not approve of something he decided, she says to us, with her husband there, "I think he should dig the garden, but he's fiddling with the computer, and he won't budge," as a way of rubbing in her point of view, of getting at him to get her way. Or he says, "B_ is at me do fix the garden gate," and he does some other job, just to prove who is boss, before he does what she asked. He's so afraid of being "controlled" by his wife that they both play games.'

Helen and Joe say they work hard to counter such moves themselves. They call it dialogue, and it isn't easy. Helen's background forbad her from expressing feelings, and as a nurse she hid them, and Joe thinks now that he was emotionally illiterate and could not even put a name to his own feelings.

'We're only together because of the grace of God,' they assure me. 'We've grown with our arms about each other. Without God we'd have walked out on marriage.'

And when I come to the end of the conversation, I think how Joe and Helen mentioned manipulation and how they try to avoid it, and my mind turns to Isaac and Rebekah in the Bible. Their marriage fell into enormous difficulty because one dominated and the other manipulated, even though Isaac genuinely loved Rebekah. The story is in Genesis 26 and 27.

Isaac and Rebekah

Isaac and Rebekah were relatives since she was the daughter of Isaac's cousin Bethuel. The marriage was arranged, at the request of Isaac's aging father Abraham, by his reliable old household manager.

Life together started most successfully. When the servant brought her to the family, Rebekah politely, and perhaps shyly, hid behind her veil while the servant told Isaac the story of the search he felt God had guided. Then Isaac took her to his mother's tent and she became his wife. 'And he loved her, and was comforted after his mother's death.' Genesis 24:67

Isaac was forty when he married Rebekah. They probably wanted children straight away. But Rebekah did not become pregnant. The Bible does not indicate how long this period was – long enough for her to acquire the label barren. Genesis 25:19 has a nice little touch (if it was done for love of Rebekah and not just in order to obtain an heir). 'Isaac prayed to the Lord for his wife, because she was barren; and the Lord granted his prayer, and his wife Rebekah conceived.'

Rebekah received knowledge from God that she would have twins, one stronger than the other, and the elder would serve the younger. But at this time Isaac and his Hebrew retainers (hardly yet a separate clan among the many desert tribes) depended heavily, like everybody else in the desert, on supplies of water for the herds and crops. Isaac's workers often competed with the workers of the local chiefs for access to water, a sensitive issue, and Isaac didn't want a fight on his hands. Yet they were forced by the water shortage to live in Gerar near petty king Abimilech and Isaac feared the local tribesmen would fight him for Rebekah because she was good looking.

So when he went to Gerar, Isaac, as his parents had done, pretended his wife was his sister. A long time later Abimelech looked out his window one day and saw Isaac fondling Rebekah. They must have been genuinely in love at that stage. Anyway when Abimelech realised their real relationship, he was irate. Someone could have taken her, another man's wife. Abimelech seemed to view a wife as a man's personal possession, but at least he wanted her to have the dignity and integrity due to her position, which was more than Isaac publicly gave her. He'd certainly failed her. In the arrangement only he gained.

But despite his lies and his highly selfish disregard for Rebekah, God blessed Isaac's household and gave such good harvests that he prospered with a large household, crops, flocks and herds. At the end of chapter 26 we find in one extra sentence some more about their family life. At age 40 Esau, the elder of their twin sons, married two women, Judith and Basemath, 'and they made life bitter for Isaac and Rebekah'.

What about Esau and Jacob?

However there are some unasked questions here. In a society where marriages were arranged, why wasn't Esau married till forty? And Jacob, now past forty, remained unmarried. Was Isaac, or were Isaac and Rebekah together, neglectful in their planning for their sons? Or could they not agree? Or, if they despised the local girls so much, why had they not arranged marriages outside? Why had Esau brought home wives who were unwelcome with his parents? Were there frequent tensions in the family between the parents? Or between parents and sons? Did they communicate well? Did they ever discuss things together? It seems not.

Mother-in-law and daughter-in-law must work very closely in a subsistence farming family – carrying water for the kitchen, planting, weeding, watering gardens, watering and feeding domestic animals, shepherding flocks, collecting firewood. Mother and daughters or daughters-in-law still do the same tasks in many countries of Asia and Africa, where approximately 70 per cent of the population are small croppers, herders like Isaac and Rebekah, or else day labourers. Perhaps Rebekah hated working with Judith and Basemath.

After the joy of their own early marriage, Isaac and Rebekah somehow failed to pass on to their sons and daughters-in-law a love and loyalty in the family. Perhaps they were not good at listening to each other. The next story shows Isaac and Rebekah each favouring one son against the other, and totally out of harmony in their old age.

The ruse of Rebekah

Isaac, elderly, with his sight failed and expecting death some time, called his favourite son Esau to take his hunting bow and arrows, shoot some game, and cook up a tasty meal before he bestowed on him the blessing for the oldest son. But Rebekah thought she knew better. The elder would serve the younger. She felt she had to try to make this happen. Perhaps if she had let God control the family, God would have engineered the right future for the brothers without her intervention.

We do not know if the couple planned things together earlier, but at this stage Isaac planned this significant act without discussing it with his wife. Rebekah only knew because she eavesdropped. She hurried to tell her other son, Jacob, her favourite,

Isaac's requests to Esau, and ordered him to go to one of the many flocks and bring two kid goats. She would make a tasty dish for him to take to Isaac before Esau returned, so he could gain the special blessing for the eldest son.

'A tall order,' thought Jacob, knowing that he didn't sound or feel like Esau. 'You know, Mother, that I'm nowhere as hairy as Esau. Father will guess and curse me instead.' But Rebekah offered to take the blame, and hurried Jacob out to the corral to get the kids for her to cook up her best recipe. She even used the goat skin to wrap his neck and hands, and slipped Esau's best clothes on to Jacob sending him to Isaac with fresh bread and the savoury, hot goat stew.

When, despite his visual handicap, Isaac tried to check which son had come, he still did not guess the ruse. He prayed the biggest blessing he could give, even that the other son would serve this one, and it fell on younger Jacob. What consternation followed when Isaac found he was deceived.

Playing games

What really happened in this family? Isaac and Rebekah were not talking. Each pushed for personal goals. And, because Isaac felt sure of his right to make the rules, he would not listen to Rebekah. She resorted to deceiving her husband. Manipulation. Playing games in people's lives, without honestly discussing and honestly working through an issue together. What might the outcome have been if Isaac and Rebekah had discussed together? How much happier the home would have been if Isaac had not dominated and Rebekah manipulated.

Now the family was unavoidably on a slippery downhill slope to self-destruct in acrimony and hatred. Esau found no substantial blessing left for him. Only something nearer a curse: to live away from the fertile fields in the desert, living by the sword against his neighbours, and likely to serve his young brother. So Esau hated Jacob and planned to wait till his father died and then kill him.

But Rebekah, skilled at listening in to conversations, heard that too, and ordered Jacob off to Haran where she came from, to escape Esau's anger. Then she needed more fast talking to explain to Isaac, to cover up to the old man who did not know what was really happening in the family.

'I'm weary of my life because of these Hittite women,' she complained to him about Judith and Basemath. 'If Jacob marries a Hittite woman like these, what good will my life be to me?'

And Isaac fell for her ploy again. He called Jacob in and gave him a traveller's blessing and a father's blessing as he hiked to his uncle Laban's place, and instructed him to marry one of the daughter's of Laban. And Esau, knowing he was out of favour because of his Hittite wives, tried to improve his standing by marrying a third woman, Mahalath, the daughter of Isaac's half brother. The Bible writer makes no comment on that move. Did Judith and Basemath vie with each other and with Mahalath for Esau's favours, or did they, as sometimes in South Asian second and third marriages today, welcome an extra hand and make her do all the work? Either way, it must have been an uncomfortable family.

Sad consequences

So Isaac lost his younger son and Rebekah her favourite son, with Jacob too afraid of Esau to return. The couple were left, Isaac still assuming he should make the rules in the family, and Rebekah hugging the secrets of her manoeuvres to try to get things her way. Major flaws in their marriage cut them off from each other. And hatred and anger between the sons split the family. Isaac and Rebekah never saw Jacob again.

What a sad example of a father-makes-the-rules-while-mother-submits, or pretends-to-submit, type of family. No wonder Joe and Helen say they abhor the manipulation they can see when couples live the stereotypes of men's and women's roles where one dominates and the other says 'Yes'.

6

Love Does Not Add Up Rights and Wrongs

Natalie and Selwyn Yeoman

Natalie and Selwyn live at the other end of New Zealand from me, and I only met them because I visited Dunedin for work. I looked for the opportunity because, with their busy church and denominational responsibilities, five growing children, Natalie's music-making in her own neighbourhood and her role as a speaker and singer-song-writer, they're something of a legend in their own day.

The 104-year-old country manse on a Friday afternoon looks unmistakably child friendly – large old trees, bicycles, running shoes, books, pets, computer, guitar, and kitchen cupboard decorated with newspaper clippings of Jude competing in national under sixteen kayaking championships. Natalie, fresh in T-shirt and red skirt, has just come in from a best-time-yet run of 39 minutes 45 seconds, as she later tells 9 year old Oliver, who often runs with her. Selwyn, wiry behind his small dark beard, comes over from the church past vigorously growing cabbages, leeks, beans and rhubarb.

We take seats on the well-worn corner furniture by the large bay window of the dining room and warm to a good discussion.

'Funny thing about equal marriage,' they exclaim right at the outset. 'We don't work at keeping everything equal. We don't, not even mentally, keep a list of who does what to make sure it balances. That's destructive. Love doesn't keep records of rights and wrongs.

'You can't quantify who has a heavier day. It's like the theological difference between law and grace. If you run your marriage by rules of who's going to do this or that, you get small-minded and petty, and annoyed with each other. What we try to do is to keep looking for ways we each can enrich or help the other.'

'We got into bad habits at one point,' Selwyn continues. 'When the children were younger, we didn't think enough about what was happening, though it's a natural drift. I was busy in parish work and we enjoyed the addition of each of our five children. It seemed natural that Natalie was engrossed in child care. Earlier Natalie was an up-front person, a music and youth leader, but home with the children she lost a lot of confidence simply by not using her public gifts.'

'It may have been just the stage of life a mother of young children passes through,' Natalie muses. 'I may not have been ready. But we should have agreed what to do rather than letting it happen. A few years later I struggled, not understanding what I had lost, to find again and use the gifts God gave me earlier.'

New Beginnings

'Another couple, our co-workers, challenged me to sing again and take lead parts. Even Selwyn couldn't do that because it would look like promoting his own wife. Lynette confronted me that if I stayed back it was mock modesty, and John prayed in a service for my creativity to be released again.'

'I was terrified, but I did my first recording only a year after that. It was called *New Beginnings*. God was teaching me to feel confident that He gave me gifts and would enable me. I took courage from two verses in 1 Peter 3, "You have become her (Sarah's) daughters as long as you do what is good and never let fears alarm you", and "Who will harm you if you are eager to do what is good? Do not fear what they fear and do not be intimidated."'

The way Selwyn and Natalie work now is a far cry from their planned ideal, they admit. They wanted a joint ministry in a church, but they found that impractical for them. Too stressful. They could never let go of their work if they were both implicated in every decision, every counselling situation and Natalie was reading over Selwyn's sermons on Saturday night to give suggestions.

'I was forever telling Selwyn what he should do,' Natalie explains. 'I was trying to live my life through him. And I wasn't always right, anyway. And after he told me a worry, he relaxed, and I kept up the worry on responsibilities that were really his. Then I'd be cross with him, agitated because he was relaxed. When we came to this parish with its huge workload eight years ago, people wanted to see us together when they asked for counselling. But that was too difficult for the family. It subordinated the children's needs to the parish, and we went to bed with everybody's problems. We felt drained and never able to switch off. We plainly had to stop working by that model.'

'We get more done separately,' Selwyn comments. 'We help each other, and of course we're together in enriching the children, but we don't do each other's work outside the family.'

Natalie now teaches music several hours a week at home and at local primary school level, and puts on musical productions in the community or the church, in addition to her own professional singing and occasional speaking engagements in any part of New Zealand. In the church she's one among several workers. Sometimes Selwyn asks her to do something if the need is for her gifts. More often she initiates, as with the children's musical she's compiled. Selwyn thinks their method takes the tensions out, and his pastoral work is separate.

A common weekend activity for all the family is to support Jude in his river kayaking competitions and triathlons by all travelling to be with him. Each of the children works on a skill encouraged by Selwyn and Natalie. Hannah at fourteen excels at dancing, Emerson, eleven, at school work, and he, Oliver and

Monica enjoy music and sport, while Monica also learns ballet. Family fun all together is to go tramping in hills or bush areas.

'Changing seasons of a family's life does make a difference,' Selwyn recognises. 'At times I used to work at the house to care for a child while Natalie was out. The first time Natalie went to Wellington to make a recording we had a friend stay to run the household, but the next time the children were all at school and I kept things going.

'This year Natalie has a very full day on Thursdays so I cook that evening meal. It was a mess at first. I was so out of practice since the days when I flatted as a student. To make a whole meal scared me and I wrote myself lists of everything I needed to do. Now it all goes smoothly. Would you like my recipe for microwave steam pudding?'

The couple works together for the needs of the children. Either would change a nappy or bath a child before bedtime when they were small, and even now the message they want the children to read is, 'We're in this together.' Whoever sees a need does it, whether vacuum cleaning or shopping, though they may discuss who has time. Natalie does most of the cleaning, but she also mows the large lawns. She has the time and likes keeping fit outdoors.

That used to be one of the demarcation disputes earlier in the marriage, they say. Natalie felt tied to the house with the children when she could not even go off for a run, or when Selwyn was away and she sacrificed all adult interests for the sake of the children. They say such disputes are rare now, after 19 years of understanding each other, adjusting and accepting each other's differences.

But the biggest hurdle in their whole marriage is only months behind them and it nearly crushed them.

Intimacy under stress

Selwyn accepted, some years previously, the respected position of co-convener of the Church's Education for Ministry Committee, which meant significant planning for the national

Presbyterian theological seminary in nearby Dunedin.The work was creative but time consuming, requiring much consultation in Dunedin and travel to other parts of New Zealand with new developments. However, deep-seated differences among staff and committee members developed into enormous tensions, requiring sometimes 30 hours a week in meetings. The other co-convener resigned. When Selwyn could put his mind on his church ministry he was already drained, and his family life was increasingly neglected.

All this came to a head with a particular decision which Natalie felt would only exacerbate an already intolerable situation. Unable any longer to support Selwyn's involvement, and attempting to maintain her role in the family, Natalie stopped taking any interest in the committee or even asking Selwyn when he came home whether it was a good meeting. But while Natalie withdrew and put more time into her music, Selwyn spent more and more time on the difficult cross-currents and pressures of the committee.

'We got to a stage where we were not talking any more,' Selwyn says. 'There were no rows, just a distance. Finally we asked, "Are we losing each other?" But kept on the same way a little longer.'

Then, as Natalie saw increasingly the anguish Selwyn was going through because of the shocking disharmony of this important denominational institute, she realised they could not stay separate. They set about rebuilding their intimacy. Natalie got caught up again in hearing about the committee's problems, but it turned out to be only for two weeks.

As the committee worked towards another important staffing recommendation, Selwyn told Natalie how the tensions were destroying his devotional life by flooding in and invading his prayer. She reminded him of the advice, 'If your foot causes you to stumble, cut it off.' When, despite the preparatory work, the committee found itself prevented from making a decision, Selwyn knew the time had come to consider resigning. But he wanted time to think about it first.

'That's where I had enough,' Natalie fills in. 'I totally put my foot down. I was prepared to write a letter of resignation myself, although of course I couldn't resign for someone else. But eventually we agreed.'

'It was hard to let go of that committee,' Selwyn adds. 'It's like running. I want to finish what I set out to do, even if I walk home. I wanted to contribute to the life of the church and to education for ministry, but in the end the demands were destroying us. If you ask where in scripture I get my ideal to aspire to in relating to Natalie, it's John 13, where Jesus put into action his willingness to serve others.'

Natalie's response to the same question turns out to be Ephesians 5, 'Be subject to one another out of reverence for Christ.' They're convinced that if one person dominates a marriage, whether the husband or the wife, trouble follows. They have seen marriages killed like that among their acquaintances.

Songs for the whole of life

It stretched both Natalie and Selwyn when Natalie's singing career took off with her records. As expected, she had to practise hard to reach a recording standard, plan the instrumental backing and backing vocals, and borrow money for the recording. The sound recordist was her brother. That helped. Then came the fan mail saying people were helped and blessed.

'I went through a crisis at that point,' Selwyn observes. 'I was glad for her and loved the album but it generated unease in me. Here Natalie was with this amazing career break and I didn't seem to be getting anywhere. I'd like to do creative things but my job puts me in a strait-jacket. It's costly and doesn't receive the short-term rewards. It's hard for a guy to keep on at a job he's done for years while his wife goes out to a new job, or higher study. He can feel trapped when his wife isn't. Just like she was trapped by the children earlier. A guy may feel threatened by his wife's ability.'

But meanwhile Natalie found in song-writing and singing an invigorating new challenge. She wrote and sang not just of devotional life but of the whole of life. Take a look at this one.

We're one of those families where the library books are always
 overdue
And when the doctor says the baby will be coming in May
We're all still waiting in June
And when we put our milk bottles out at the gate
The milk truck is just pulling out of our street
But when you return Lord we're gonna be ready for you

The very pressures of being a minister's wife, a professional in her song-writing and musicianship, and feeling bathed in the love of a husband and five children became the stuff of Natalie's writing in this song to her children.

I'm grabbing time to write my songs
That's the way it has to be
I live my life just grabbing on to you
And your love grabs hold of me.

Now the telephone is ringing. 'No I'm sorry he's not home
But can I take a message? Yes I'm sure he'll be back soon.'
And now the baby's waking up. Uh-oh I've got a hunch
That though it's nearly time for tea she hasn't had her lunch.

Now I have to get up earlier to keep one step ahead
But I must admit for privacy there's no place like our bed
I'm knee deep in nappies but I'm head-high in love
And I don't know where I'd be without these 'blessings' from above.

Small wonder people want this practical and warm mother as speaker when they need to learn more about equality for women in society and home while giving warmth to family life and fun. With the BA, LLB degrees she won in her student days, Natalie is well placed to analyse what she learns of the life of women. She accepts invitations to groups all over the country, and one of her next assignments is lectures to a conference of evangelical university students. Her own story of regaining confidence is a natural teaching vehicle. So are her devotional and family songs.

Oh make each house a home, a place where each may grow to be
the person that you want, strong and kind, and ready to see
how to shoulder one another's loads, and
feel each others pains and sorrows
Making peace before the sun goes down
beginning new each morning again.

One could say that, in the same way that Natalie does, the prophets in Bible times spoke about the whole of life. Their messages were about practical human relationships like concern for the poor, like getting on with other people. In this sense Natalie and Selwyn may be treading in the footsteps of Deborah and Lappidoth, whom we want to look at for our Bible study in this chapter.

Deborah and Lappidoth

Deborah the judge

When the people of Israel were new immigrants to Canaan, settled, but still carving for themselves a customary ownership of land, they had no king, no chief, and not even a non elected assembly or bureaucracy. It was an unstable existence, few leaders, no law enforcement, and open to attacks from the tribes they were displacing. Not comfortable.

The Israelite tribes, barely united by their ancestors and their religion, and fragmented by the mountains, made little effort to support each other in the conflicts for control of land. Tribal connections were breaking down and the Israelites were losing ground against their foes.

In the crises that followed, a series of judges became the nearest thing the tribes had to a political ruler – men like Gideon and Samson. Their success, measured in two areas, required enormous personal skills: judging the civil disputes between Israelites, and uniting the Israelites enough to stand against their enemies, or even be known as united enough to deter their enemies from attack.

At the time of the crisis described in Judges 4 the Israelites needed a commander to lead them against King Jabin of Canaan and his general Sisera, but none came forward. They cried to the Lord for help because Sisera could amass against them nine hundred chariots of iron, while the Israelites did not even know how to make iron! Worse still, the Canaanites controlled the main valleys and trade routes and prevented the Israelites from moving freely north and south. Yet most Israelites, tenaciously independent, hated the thought of a king. They would rather manage their disputes through a series of judges, and this is where Deborah comes in.

Deborah was already recognised as a religious prophet and a civilian judge, though we have no background on how she, the first woman so described in Israel, came to receive the role. Her task at this stage was to set up court under a palm tree between Ramah and Bethel in the south of the territory of the tribe of Ephraim. When people had a difference, strong enough to need a mediator or judge to give a verdict, they took their case to Deborah for her to hear and judge between them.

She must have been effective. Her authority was so well recognised that she could give instructions that would motivate Barak and eventually the fighting men of two tribes (and later another four tribes mentioned in Judges 6) to turn out for battle.

For our purposes, because Deborah was a married woman, we shall try to pick out something of the way of operating that Deborah and Lappidoth must have practised. Since we gather from Judges 5:31 that Deborah ruled Israel for a further 40 years, we can suppose she was young, perhaps in her twenties at the time. Being a prophet and a judge was a highly responsible position for a young adult and probably not without considerable job stresses. And if Deborah was like most young married women of the time, she would have young children as well.

We wonder what sort of man Lappidoth was. In his twenties also? A landowner with a palm tree on the road side? He seems to be quite happy for his wife to serve God and the nation as prophet and judge. We can hardly imagine how the couple felt the first time God gave Deborah a prophecy, as they grappled with the change in their position in the neighbourhood and in the tribe. Lappidoth must have supported Deborah's new role and accepted that she had an authority he did not have. After all, being a prophet meant representing God to the people. God's ambassador. That was a big deal.

Perhaps the couple had to make arrangements for the children when Deborah was out at her work as a judge. Perhaps Lappidoth stayed with the children, or a relative or serving woman lived in with the family, or perhaps the couple lived in an extended family with others who could absorb the children into the running of their own family.

Holding two important roles

Really Deborah had two tasks, a spiritual one as prophet to represent God to the Israelites, and a secular one as judge to settle disputes between the people and look after the foreign relations of the tribe in place of a king.

The roles look terribly important. In view of the fact that we were taught so long that God always wants men to be the leaders, and husbands to head up every home, we wonder why God did not choose Lappidoth for the task.

The answer I was told in church was that when men fail to lead, then God chooses women. Many women can accept this if their husband is a gifted man and they do not believe they have gifts themselves, though it tends to make women think they do not have a gift. But for some couples and single women it is a most awkward teaching. It means that when a woman takes up a call from God to do a task that is outside a private arena of the home, she implies a criticism of her husband, or, if she is a single woman with a public or church calling, she in effect criticises all the men in that sphere because she would imply that they had failed. But women who know that it is a Christian grace not to put themselves ahead of others, do not want to do that. The easy way out is to try not to hear God's call to a new level of public Christian service.

Deborah did not seem to be faced with any worry that she was stepping in front of her husband or implying a criticism of him. And God went right ahead and gave her public tasks. We can only conclude that God chose to give the task to a woman, and gave her the gifts she needed to carry it out.

Deborah the prophet

The next job was to motivate and work with the man who should be general of the army, feeding courage into him for the task. Deborah sent for Barak to tell him Jehovah's message, a specific prophecy, 'God commands you, take up a position at Mount Tabor, bringing ten thousand from the tribe of Naphtali and the tribe of Zebulun . . . I will give Sisera into your hand.'

Barak's reply came back, 'If you will go with me, I will go; but if you will not go with me, I will not go.'

For the first time we have in Deborah's answer a hint of a comment on men's roles and women's roles when it comes to fighting physical battles. 'I will surely go with you; nevertheless, the road on which you are going will not lead to your glory, for the Lord will sell Sisera into the hand of a woman.'

So Deborah went with Barak to Kedesh to call the army and then went out with him to fight. And we may think, 'Look at that! Lappidoth and Deborah must have had a very good understanding of each other in their marriage.' He had such faith in her that he understood her going off on a journey with another man, helping him head up, of all things, an army. She knew he trusted her so thoroughly that she did not even seem to discuss with him what she felt God was telling her to do next. Perhaps they had already talked much and understood the call of God on their lives, before anything about fighting battles for the nation came into their lives.

The story tells us that when Sisera heard that Barak and his troops had gone to Mount Tabor, he called out his nine hundred chariots and all his troops. As they approached, Deborah gave the pre-battle motivational pep talk to Commander Barak. 'Up!

For this is the day on which the Lord has given Sisera into your hand. The Lord is indeed going out before you.'

Taking Deborah at her word, Barak set off down the mountain with his ten thousand men. Sisera's army panicked, they were slain by the sword and not a man was left. Just as Deborah's prophecy said, Sisera, fled on foot and taking refuge in the tent of a woman called Jael, he was killed in a dastardly move by his hostess.

In the joy of victory Deborah voiced one of the longest prophetic songs in the whole Bible, with verses and antiphonal questions from a choir of singers. She and Barak sang their praise to God for their amazing success. They gave credit to the people who offered themselves willingly and to the Lord who answered their need. And the people praised Deborah and Barak and Jael and told the story over and over.

A remarkable postscript follows this story of how Deborah motivated a whole army. 'The land had rest for forty years.' It is not spelt out exactly why peace lasted so long after the battle. Perhaps Deborah's work stood the test of four decades because she and Barak had successfully, with God's help, quelled the neighbouring opposition to the Israelites. Perhaps she successfully united the tribes of Israel. And yet again, perhaps Deborah ruled so well as internal judge that tiffs and disputes between the people ceased.

What a remarkable couple Lappidoth and Deborah were. A couple led by God who, for the nation and for God, used her gifts of leadership and his team work to support her as judge and prophet for their nation. They took it further and included Barak and the army in their team work. They served well both their generation and their God.

7

Moving Together, and Room to Move

When forgiving comes first

One of the times Brian and I agreed about a major decision was when we bought our house in Auckland.

That was the year we spent in New Zealand not far from Brian's mother. He was lecturing at Auckland Technical Institute and also studying the final five papers for his Bachelor of Divinity, while we lived in a rented house. A letter one morning galvanised us into trying to buy a house, even though we planned to return to India. The letter from Brian's brother and his wife contained a cheque for a deposit on a house. A house of our own! If we let it while we were away, the rent could cover the mortgage.

We scraped around our little savings accounts from our teaching before we departed for India nearly six years before and added Brian's earnings that year. Yes, we could now reach the deposit. Together we wrote a seven-point list of our requirements in a house, things like low enough price, big enough for a family of five, room for a study, a garage for a car, and not so old that it would need maintenance when we were away from New Zealand.

Brian was teaching by day and studying for final exams in the evenings, so it fell to me to make the first appraising decisions of what was available. I could easily go out to house hunt – well sort of easily. I'll admit I felt grossly encumbered when real estate agents called to take me to view houses – I had to bundle lively four-year-old Kaaren into the car, then two year old Bronwyn, followed by my bulky nine months pregnant self!

I studied the newspaper each morning, called agents, visited houses for a week and a half, deciding they were too expensive, too old, too small or too dangerously near a stream for a young family. In the evenings I described the houses to Brian and by the weekend we felt pushed for time. His exams were coming up. My confinement was overdue. We prayed hard.

On Tuesday an agent phoned to tell me of a house that sounded likely. I saw it on a Wednesday. Real possibilities. Built on a slope below the road, room to excavate for a basement, three bedrooms, an iron roof, weatherboard that needed paint, and a price within our budget. No garage, but extra room if we dug out the spoil on the slope for a basement. Must bring Brian back to see this one.

However, Brian took me to the maternity hospital in the early hours of the next morning, 13th September, and baby Adrienne greeted the world before breakfast. I stopped thinking much about a new house. I had other things on my mind.

But Brian, having taken the day off work with the new addition to the family, went to see the house, liked it, took his mother along to get her opinion, and started negotiating a price that was three thousand dollars less than we expected to pay. That evening he came to the maternity hospital with the papers to sign for joint ownership.

Our own home. We could put the picture hooks where we wanted on the walls. Take snapshots of the girls on the front path so that when we went back to India we could show them the photos and say, 'This is our home in New Zealand. This is our family's base. We'll go home one day, and your bedroom will still be there.'

Years later I found the card with our seven specifications. Brian had written on it 'Praise the LORD 14/9/73.'

Agreeing about decisions

Now I look back I see how we discussed and agreed on the decisions, or where it was practical for one person to decide, that one did. But there is an oddity about that, because at the time we believed, because it was such a strong part of our Christian culture, that Brian had to be the head of the family and make all major decisions.

In actual situations we each respected the other's judgment and most often made joint decisions. And when we wanted guidance from God for a major decision, we prayed together and each individually prayed and searched for the right answer as well.

In other situations we let the one who knew most about a subject make a decision in that area. Choosing a piano when Brian was the musician was obviously his task, likewise sport, or anything to do with running the school. I looked after family purchases and regular shopping, though we both agreed on a conscious simple lifestyle.

One morning as I brushed my hair an idea dropped into my head that I think came from God. Kaaren was ten and about to go to the boarding school in south India where we used to teach. Now I wondered if she should stay at the tiny school in Pokhara, Nepal, longer and not go south till she had to when she was nearly eleven. Brian left it all to me to arrange. That turned out to be Kaaren's last few months with her father and very important.

Sometimes initiatives depended simply on who had time. Choosing how to spend leisure time was one of the joint tasks, till I realised that Brian was so pressured during the Sunday to Friday working week that he could not put thought into friends to spend time with on Saturdays, the one day free after church finished at 9.00a.m. There were no phones. I used to suggest friends to Brian and write a note on Monday to have a reply later in the week as to whether they could come walking with us on Saturday.

We did not plan it, but the same pattern began to affect spiritual leading. Because we thought a man always leads in spiritual things, Brian always led the Sunday evening study when it was our turn to host the English language Bible study for the eight foreign families based at the school. But one Sunday when our colleagues were coming, Brian had heavy stresses on at the school with no chance at all to prepare, while I had all day free as I stayed with the children. I did the obvious thing, prepared the study and led in the evening. None of the wives had done such a thing. And without discussing our swap in roles, Brian, surprised, concentrated on settling the children into bed.

Without analysing it, we often unwittingly practised an equal marriage while thinking we had to conform to a pattern of leader and follower. I wonder now if there are other couples who do the same.

But of course decisions, and who makes them, don't always go so smoothly.

Trekking right or wrong

The Nepali summer was in full force one July school holiday as we set out to trek to the base of Annapurna II. In my view, the razor back ridge is one of the most beautiful mountains in all Nepal.

Brian had his large old backpack with light sleeping bags and a borrowed tent. I had stuffed into mine a half pillowcase of clothes for each of us and my newly concocted muesli of local beaten rice, coconut, brown sugar and milk powder. Kaaren, Bronnie and Adrienne, each in their T-shirts and homemade shorts, were big enough to walk in their rubber chappals (thongs), while Brian slung little Rosi up on his shoulders above the grey pack.

Well into learning to talk, she practised repeating the days of the week after her father, 'Sunday, Monday, Tuesday, Sunday, Monday, Tuesday, what's next, Daddy?'

'Say it after me, Rosi. Tuesday, Wednesday, Thursday. I'm taking you on a short cut I've worked out,' Brian continued to me as we splashed through the watercourse at the edge of a paddy field, he in boots and socks, me in plastic sandals because the weather was so sticky hot. 'The usual route to Siklis village, starting on the other side of Pokhara town, takes 12 hours. Most people allow one and a half days. But we're cutting back from the northern side. We'll do it much quicker.'

'But, how's that Brian? Nobody else goes that way.'

'Oh, I've worked it out. We'll only need to go over one low range of hills.'

'Show it to me on the map, dear.'

'Oh, don't worry. We won't need a detailed map. I went to Siklis one other time, so I can work out how to go from this side.'

Under my breath I wasn't so sure about this taking off across the ranges of terraced rice fields and forest without checking out the regular route, but Brian was the expert on mountains and maps. I let it go.

Dragonflies danced glittering in front of us, bronze, navy blue and glinting green beetles whirred and crawled, variegated spiders hung their threads across the narrow clay trail. All the brilliance of insect life comes out in the monsoon weather. But so did the jugas (leeches).

'Wait for me, Dad. I've got two jugas on my arm.'

'Wait on. I'm trying to get them off but there's three more on my legs while I'm standing here. Look, Dad.'

'Now it's raining, Mum. It doesn't matter if we haven't got umbrellas, does it? And we couldn't stand raincoats in this heat. We'll dry easily. It's so hot.'

'Here we are, up over this hill. I'll help you up this slippery bit on the path,' Brian calls out to the girls, while we wander on tiny field paths. We weave among pocket handkerchiefs of rice terraces, stopping all the time for leeches. The tiny black worms sneakily inject an anticoagulant that stops the blood from clotting. When, stuffed with our blood and fat as slugs, they drop off, the tiny wounds bleed profusely. Our legs are streaked with red.

'Twenty-one, twenty-two, twenty-three. I've picked twenty-three leeches off,' seven-year-old Bronnie counts gleefully. 'We've come to "jugadesh", the land of leeches.'

We ask the name of the large village. Never heard of it. We're slowing down and the children are tired. What, another range, more villages, more rice terraces, more patches of jungle. Oh, well, we can ask for floor space in a house here for the night. On again the next day.

'Monday, Tuesday, Wednesday,' sings Rosi.

'Fifty-four, fifty-five, fifty-six leeches,' chants Bronnie, and when there are no villagers around, our perspiring young progeny strip off to their knickers and splash in the irrigation streams beside the fields.

'Range number three,' I think near the end of the second day, as we seek floor space again in a village on a hill. The children are crying from tiredness and disappointment.

But next morning Rosi crows again from her perch on Brian's shoulders, 'Tuesday, Wednesday, Thursday.'

'Eighty-nine, ninety, ninety-one,' continues Bronnie, as we trudge into Siklis after two and a half days. We are up under magnificent Annapurna II, but it is hidden behind the clouds. It has been such hard going – loads, leeches, monsoon mist, heat, hills. If only Brian had not taken us on a dead-loss short cut. We walk home on the correct path – only one range, a walking path a whole metre wide, no leeches, and only one and a half days.

There's no point in grumbling at Brian. He made a mistake, but complaining will not help. I accept his decision and live with the consequences. You give each other room to move, room to make mistakes. You forgive. It makes relating much smoother. I had cause to be glad that Brian gave me room for mistakes when I made a major blunder a few months later.

Forgiving

The picture this time is Parents' Day at the Gandaki Boarding School where Brian is principal. Not many parents from the surrounding hills can make the two or three-day trip but there are scores of local officials and friends of the school and the boys are keyed up for their many competitions in sports, traditional dance and academic subjects. The biggest event of the day is the individual and group projects that have been prepared during several weeks – science, literature, geography, language, history, art, agriculture. There are even three entries in Western classical music. One boy, I think his name may have been Amar Singh, had gone to enormous trouble to learn from Brian the Western musical scale and script and written out pieces and prepared tapes of his singing and playing in classical musical style on a guitar.

Brian asked me as the headmaster's wife, to impartially judge this important part of the programme, because I usually had little to do with the school and would not be biased towards boys I knew. Busily I moved among the over 40 entries from the senior boys. Impressive. Only the hardest working boys bothered entering, and these had done extremely well. Some even entered in rabbit keeping with healthy rabbits in strong bamboo cages on clean sawdust. I wrote down a grade for each aspect – content, language, illustrations, presentation. Judging took nearly two hours.

I added up the grades for each aspect and gave Brian a list of First, Second, Third, and two highly commended. He announced the winners and gave out the prizes, and the day drew to a comfortable close as the boys left for the Dasain festival holidays.

Late that afternoon Brian and I discussed the competition.

'Splendid work they did,' I tell him. 'I was impressed. They don't have the resources of a school in the West, but the standard they reached was extraordinary.'

'Did you see Amar Singh's music project?' he asked.

'Oh, yes. That was outstanding,' I answer. 'It was among the highest scoring. I think that was first, wasn't it?'

'No. You didn't mention it in the list.'

'Oh, it must have been second then. I'll look on the paper I was working on again.'

'But you didn't mention it at all.'

'What! Let me add these up again. Oh, Brian. This is dreadful. I missed his when I was adding up the final scores. He had the highest score. He should have won.'

I was so ashamed of my mistake. I still feel bad 15 years later when I think about it. Brian trusted me to do a task and I failed him, and let down one of the most able boys in the school.

The funny thing was, Brian didn't even reproach me. I would have deserved it if he had ranted at me long and hard, but he hardly said a thing. From his own pocket he quickly arranged a prize for Amar Singh, talked to the Nepalese dean of studies, and talked to Amar privately. He could not unseat the proclaimed winner in any way, but I do not think he even told Amar the mistake was my fault.

Looking back, I realise Brian tried to do what was right, but also simply accepted that I had made a mistake. And I knew again the importance of being forgiven.

Forgiving is basic. I could think myself patient for not grumbling at Brian when he led us on a trek that was much too badly planned and exhausting for our young family, but I forgave. I needed him to forgive me at times, like my mistake with marking the projects.

I grew to love the bit in 2 Corinthians 4 about humans holding the treasure of the goodness of God in clay jars. If any good comes, it is from God, not from us. And if our friend, or husband or wife, makes a major mistake, we acknowledge they are made of clay and forgive because we want them to forgive us too, if we mess something up, because we are only clay jars too.

I have this in mind as I turn to our next Bible study – the story of Manoah and his wife. They moved together, talked events over together, one took responsibility for areas that one alone needed to handle, and when one made a mistake, the other could put the picture right with no recriminations. The story is in Judges 13, recording the time God told the parents of Samson they would have a son.

The Parents of Samson

Samson foretold

Among the judges who ruled Israel after Deborah, some were honest and some were not, some were successful, some were failures: Gideon, Tola, Jair, Jephthah. Between the years ruled by judges the people drifted, disorganised and turning often to other gods. When they did this, God allowed them to be harassed or conquered by their enemies. The judges who became national heroes did so because they fought the Israelites' oppressors and regained for Israel their national pride.

When this story opens, the Israelites are again in trouble with God for their evil actions, and God has let them be forced to pay tribute to the king of the Philistines for the last 40 years. The next judge would be Samson.

In the territory of the tribe of Dan, a woman whose name we do not know, Manoah's wife, lived with the sadness of being barren. One day she came face to face with an angel. Not an ordinary angel either, but **the** angel of the Lord, which usually means in the Bible, God himself in the form he used as a messenger.

'Although you're barren,' said the angel, 'you're going to become pregnant and have a son. There are some rules with this because he's going to be special. Don't drink any wine or strong drink, don't eat anything ritually unclean, and never, never shave or cut the boy's hair. He's going to be set apart as a Nazirite, a man chosen by God to carry out his wishes. He's the one who'll begin to deliver Israel from control by the Philistines.'

Perhaps she whispered, 'Wow, and whacky doo,' under her breath. It was almost too good to be true. Her! A son! She hurried to tell her husband.

'Manoah, listen. A man of God came and talked to me. He was so startling I think he was an angel of God. Awesome. I didn't ask where he came from and he didn't tell me his name, but he said, "You're going to become pregnant and have a son. Don't drink wine or strong drink or eat anything unclean. The boy's going to be a Nazirite from the day he's born till the day he dies." '

Manoah wants his own angel visit

Manoah was not a young man. He and his wife had been married long enough, childless, for her to attract the label 'barren' in their neighbourhood. Now he wanted to know for himself what was happening. He had only her word of the angel's instructions.

'O Lord,' he prayed, 'let the man of God you sent to my wife come again and teach us what we are to do about the boy.'

He might have felt confused by the turn of events. Anyway God took pity on Manoah and sent the angel back again, but surprisingly, to his wife, and not to Manoah who had asked for the visit. This time the good woman was sitting in the field. Perhaps she had paused from hoeing the barley. She knew her husband needed some convincing. Here was her opportunity.

She raced off and called to Manoah, 'Come quick! The man who gave me the message the other day has come back.'

Manoah had to get up to follow his wife. Was he on his knees weeding the cucumbers?

'Are you the man who spoke to my wife?' he asked.

'I am.'

Manoah stuttered out a question he had already heard the answer to, but he wanted to hear it for himself. 'If your words come true, what are the rules about this boy's upbringing? What are we to do? What's he to do?'

Patiently the angel ran again through the deal he had given. 'Your wife's got the instructions. She needs to be sure to keep them. He's not to eat grapes or anything unclean, nor drink wine or strong drink. I've given the instructions to her.'

At last Manoah had heard it for himself. He felt secure. Still not realising this was the angel of the Lord, he offered to get a feast ready for the visitor, but no, the visitor would not eat, though he would accept a sacrifice.

Manoah killed a kid and made a hearty meal, but the thought was teasing the back of his mind, 'A sacrifice? Who accepts sacrifices? Only God?' He asked his visitor, 'What is your name?' The visitor fobbed him off with an indirect answer but there was more to come. When Manoah put the meat on a rock in front of the guest, it burst into flame and the angel disappeared towards heaven in the flames while the astounded couple fell on their faces in the field in amazement.

Manoah grows afraid

The next thing that happened was that Manoah lost his cool. 'We're going to die, my dear. We'll die. We've seen God and if a person sees God they always die,' he whimpered.

But his wife did not so easily fear. 'Think hard, Manoah. If God wanted to kill us, he could have. If he was angry with us he'd never have accepted our offering of grain and meat and burnt it in the flame. And, what's more, God wouldn't have told us these instructions, if we were going to die. Well, anyway, I don't expect to die in the next nine months if I'm going to have a child.'

And sure enough, the prophecy came true. They had a son named Samson, the blessing of God was on him and the increased measure of the spirit of the Lord stirred him to amazing feats.

Manoah and his wife

Looking back over the account we see a strong relationship between Manoah and his wife. She was as anxious as he for Manoah to know about the visit from the angel. But Manoah was puzzled that the angel called on his wife and not on him. He really wanted to know what was happening, and he did not think the message adequately given unless it came to him.

But that was not the view of the angel of the Lord. When the wife needed the instructions because she would carry them out, she received the instructions first. This was not the way things were normally done. Men expected to have the knowledge and give the orders in the family. That was why Manoah wanted the instructions to come to him. But the angel kept it brief when he ran through the list for Manoah. As he commented, he had already told the wife.

We are forced to conclude that, even though Manoah saw himself as the one who ran the household, God communicated with the wife because she was the one who needed the rules more than the husband. The responsibility rested on her. God in the shape of an angel made this clear by appearing both times to the wife, and responding to Manoah only to humour his curiosity. Both the task and the accountability belonged, surprisingly for Manoah, to his wife.

And right to the end it was the wife who kept her head. When, despairing, Manoah thought he and his wife would die, it was his wife who had the wit to grasp the implications of what had happened and allay his fears that Jehovah God would punish him forthwith for his sins.

The story of Manoah and his wife, when God wanted them to know they would have a son, tells us that God expected a wife to be directly accountable to him for carrying out his orders to the family. There was never a hint that she was to report to her husband as if she was further down the pecking order. Neither was there a suggestion that Manoah should get the orders from God and pass them to his family.

I gain the impression at the beginning of the story when the wife was so eager to tell Manoah about the angel that the couple moved together, understood each other and had a good relationship. She was not trying to become more dominant. But they did not live in each other's pockets. The wife worked in one field, Manoah in another. Each took responsibility for his or her own area on the farm. God was teaching them to do it in planning their lives as well.

8

Cheques and Choices

Annabel's Story

I often make friends with other women who are bringing up children on their own so that was how I came to meet Annabel, though she's much younger than I.

When her marriage collapsed, she told me, the biggest problem had been the decisions about finances and property. We chatted at her flat one Saturday evening while twenty month old Sonya, in the way of all toddlers, called on Annabel (neither are their real names) to play, to read stories, and to bring cups of milk – anything to keep from going to bed.

Annabel's looks back

When Nigel and I got married we were both in our early twenties, both students. Shortly afterwards I finished my course and got a good job in the international finance section of one of New Zealand's largest exporting companies. A year later Nigel also graduated and got a job. Since we were both earning, we could buy our first home when we were twenty-three and twenty-four.

Nigel said early on that he would make the decisions on finance, and I accepted that because that's how things were in the family where I grew up – father made the decisions.

The problems started with small things. When my parents gave us a replacement stove because our old one was broken, we put out the old one, but Nigel had determined that we would not pay for an electrician to hook up the new one. That was okay, but he delayed doing it himself. For weeks I cooked whole meals in an electric frying pan, while he refused to let me get an electrician.

Nigel wanted to outdo all his friends financially. His models were uncles who were successful businessmen, and he wanted to be a millionaire too.

Not long after we bought our own house, he decided to go for rental property and bought some flats without even talking it over with me, though he expected me to work with him on cleaning and redecorating them for tenants. Then it was another house and another. Of course we didn't have enough money for all this. He told lies in the application to the bank manager the first time, and kept doing so. And we had a mammoth mortgage.

I was desperately unhappy with all this, but I felt I had to comply. Peace at any price. Though I had earned half the money, my say was invalid. I felt I was invisible for all the mark my opinion made on Nigel's life.

How did this happen? I had better passes from university than Nigel, and in my job I was working with finance, but suddenly it was his domain. I had fallen back to the role my mother had. My mother always took a back seat position, even if she physically did the running round paying the bills. My Dad bought the family car without even consulting with her.

I should have been forewarned of Nigel's family's view of a wife. I heard his brother say before we were married that all a wife does is spend your money. The brothers resented their mother's expenses, even for something as important as new reading glasses. I didn't let myself give it any significance at the time. I was infatuated into thinking it wouldn't matter.

During our first year of marriage, when I was working and Nigel was studying, I would get home late at the end of the day, and though he was at home he would not make the evening meal. I did it, and that seemed normal, the way things should be. My mother always did all cooking, washing, cleaning, putting the rubbish out, gardening. But she had not been out all day earning as well.

We continued the same pattern when Nigel and I were both working similar hours – that is, I did all the housework, cooking and laundry. When I told Nigel I was unhappy with this, he just did nothing. He saw no need to change.

And I knew no way to mark out what I wanted, to change what was happening. I did not ask anyone for advice, nor read for ideas. Because of my upbringing, part of me said, 'This is right and normal,' but part of me shouted, 'This is not sense. It's not fair!' But I did not let myself think about it. In fact for years I denied the problem .

We both grew up in conservative churches. We believed the biblical example was husbands making all the major decisions. Full stop. I did not ask advice at church. Anyway church would say I should submit to Nigel. If Nigel thought about it, he would have thought it was working out fine. It just did not work for me, nor for my ethical principles.

I grew increasingly upset about Nigel's business ethics, too. He kept telling lies and he utterly refused to make a tax declaration. He did not fill in a tax return for years. If we had paid taxes, no way could we have gone on buying properties.

I felt divorced from my own principles. My conscience whispered, 'You've done these things you don't agree with,' until I did not want to live with myself. My inner self was quite separate from my external self. I felt paralysed.

Eventually, one year when the Inland Revenue Department was offering a tax amnesty that forgave penalties for overdue taxes, I decided to act. I created a set of accounts from sketchy financial records. I asked Nigel's help, but he brushed me aside. Then I put the returns in, as I had told him I would. He beat me up.

I felt responsible for both his and my decisions. It was not till later that I realised that I was not responsible for him. I could not change him. But also he was not responsible for me.

For the present I had a shocking conscience, so bad I was ill. I overate, I indulged in chocolates, my work suffered because I could not concentrate, and I sat knitting for hours. I knitted so long I wrecked my hands with carpal tunnel syndrome (repetitive strain injury). I remember when our trees overhung the property of a neighbour who asked us to trim them. Nigel would not, so I tried, but I could not work the little saw any longer.

Soon I was a cot case – so bad that Mum and Dad came to look after me. When they arrived the house was a mess, I could not even get out of bed to get food for myself, and Nigel had gone fishing. They stayed some days and then inadvertently added to my trauma. My Dad suffered a heart attack and died in front of me. My world fell apart.

I had for years kept up a brave face. I believed I was married for life. Nigel did not often hit me physically, but he hit me with his tongue, with verbal abuse so persistent I felt incapacitated. I had never been socially adept at communicating, and did not know how to defend myself with words or any other way.

It took me ages to figure out what was going wrong. Trust had broken down. I read the whole New Testament looking for meaning in life. I tried to apply Jesus' words so I could trust my husband, but there was no trust. He dominated me, he became unfaithful to me, and I could not live with his financial deals.

He did start by making money, but it was ill-gotten gain, morally wrong, and later his deals did not work because he didn't pay for financial advice, or maintenance on the properties, or rent collection. He was still employed in a full-time job, but the company did not get value from him. He did not put in the time. Buying properties became addictive with him – it buried the pain of his sense of failure if he did not make a lot of money. He would buy another property and I only learnt about it afterward.

He bought a bed and breakfast hotel, telling the bank manager when he took a loan, that I would be doing all the room care and cleaning. Nigel did not even ask me. And how could I do it? I was already off work with a severe stress related allergy that immobilised me.

Even then it took another three years before I decided to leave my husband when our little daughter was just a few months old. On the day I bought a push chair to take Sonya about and Nigel roundly abused me for spending the money, my mind took a new turn almost without my leave. It said, 'No, I don't need a new push chair. I need a new husband.'

I thought long and hard and one March day I packed up Sonya's and my clothes, left a note, and headed for my mother and then a flat of our own six hundred kilometres away in Auckland.

Looking back, I might as well have been writing my own soap opera, the outrageous relationship I put up with in those ten years. I have no intention of getting into soap opera again.

The question of assets

Decisions about money and assets were what went wrong for Annabel. Yet while she thought she could make no decisions, she did decide. She decided she would comply with Nigel's actions, because she believed it was beyond her control to influence what was happening.

It is on this point that she could perhaps have initially received help. Her actions may have been different if she had known she was, whether she intended it or not, making decisions about their money. She was afraid of Nigel anyway, but it never occurred to Annabel to explain clearly and firmly that she could not continue supporting the wild spending and would start another bank account for her money if necessary.

The further factor that bound her to inaction was the culture and teaching of home and church that in her mind and Nigel's gave him the right to run the finances of the family with no reference to her, even if his decisions were bad both economically and ethically.

Here again Nigel and Annabel could have received help. If they had realised that in the Bible God applauded the action of a woman who took the decision into her own hands when her difficult husband made bad decisions on use of money or assets, perhaps they could have acted differently.

Abigail and Nabal

This story is found in 1 Samuel 25. Before David became king, at a time when he commanded a guerrilla band of six hundred men ranging the hills of Judea, his men were very good to the servants and three thousand sheep and one thousand goats of a wealthy grazier called Nabal. The guerrillas protected both men and stock so well that they were like a wall round them. So when David heard that Nabal was shearing his sheep, which meant there was plenty of food around to feed the shearers, he sent ten young men.

'Peace be to you,' they said, 'and peace be to your house, and peace be to all that you have. I hear you have shearers. We've looked after your shepherds and your livestock. Ask your shepherds if it's true. We'd be pleased if you gave us a reward for our trouble, like some of the feast you've got for your shearers.'

But Nabal, who was a surly fellow, and mean, answered, 'Who is David? Servants these days often leave their masters. Shall I give my bread and the meat I've butchered for my shearers to men I don't even know?'

So David's followers reported the insult back to David, who told all his men to strap on their swords, and, leaving two hundred to guard their camp, he took four hundred to attack Nabal's ranch.

Unexpectedly one of Nabal's men heard about the planned ambush and hurried over to talk with Abigail saying, 'You need to know about this. The murderous plot will kill Nabal and all the rest of us, yet Nabal is so stubborn he won't listen to anyone.'

Abigail did not say much. Perhaps she was too busy, or perhaps she did not want to talk to the servants about her husband's bad temper, but she certainly acted. She collected two hundred loaves of bread, two skin bottles of wine, five butchered sheep, five bushels of pop corn, one hundred bunches of raisins and two hundred cakes of figs, loaded them on to donkeys and commanded her young men, 'You go on in front. I'm on the way behind you.' She said never a word to bad-tempered Nabal.

When Abigail rode on a donkey round the side of the mountain, meeting David and his guerrillas coming towards her, he had been saying, probably through clenched teeth, 'What's the good of my protecting all the livestock on the grazing land of that good-for-nothing Nabal? He didn't lose a single animal, yet when I ask for a little payment, he insults me. May God strike me dead if I leave even one of his men alive till tomorrow morning.'

Down jumped lively Abigail from her donkey. In front of David she fell on her face, bowing right down to the ground, and pleading.

'Let the blame fall on me, sir. Please, let me talk this over with you. Don't take Nabal seriously. He's as bad-tempered as his name and talks utter nonsense. The reply would have been much different, but I didn't personally get a chance to talk to those first ten scouts you sent.

'Please sir, you know we both believe in God, and he hasn't let you spill blood yet. I wish you well. I've even brought this present for you to give a feast to your merry men. Please forgive Nabal's crass stupidity. I know God will certainly make you win in your battles because you are fighting on God's side and you always do it right. If anyone set out to catch you out and get rid of you, they'd fail because God looks after you. But God will throw out all your enemies. Eventually when God helps you become king of Israel, you'll have a clear conscience, because you won't have shed innocent blood, if you listen to my plea for our household and our workers. When God's finished making you win through, don't forget to be kind to us.'

Abigail's amazing action shocked David into changing his mind. Her initiative totally turned him round till he exclaimed, 'What a wonderful God we have, who has sent you to meet me today. Thank God for your good sense, and what a happy thing it is that you kept me today from the guilt of shedding blood. God stopped me from hurting you. If you hadn't hurried down here, not one of Nabal's men would be alive in the morning.' And as David accepted the gifts she brought, he said,'Go back up the mountain to your home in peace. I won't kill your husband or any of your workers.'

So Abigail climbed back up the mountain and found Nabal had thrown a feast fit for a king. Since he was roaring drunk, she said nothing, and went to bed. Only when he was sober next morning did Abigail tell her husband the narrow escape they all had.

The shock to Nabal was enormous, or was it a shock from God? Nabal suffered a major stroke and lay as if his heart was stone for the next ten days and then died. The Bible says God killed him.

Of course the news drifted down to David. 'Isn't God extraordinarily good to me!' he exclaimed. 'He's punished Nabal for his insults, and brought his bad behaviour back on his own head, while saving me from the guilt of killing another.'

Next thing, David realised he would appreciate such a wise woman himself and set about winning Abigail over to be his wife. That seems a bit sudden to us. But Abigail would not be permitted by Israelite law to inherit the family ranch and could not even stay on in the house even though they were a wealthy family. Women could not own property. She had to be attached to a husband. And David wanted her.

She went off meekly with David's messengers, riding her donkey and accompanied by her five women servants. Apparently it was a great privilege to be married to David, though looking at the arrangement from the viewpoint of the twentieth century, we may have our doubts about joining an already incumbent wife, Ahinoam.

A Woman of worth

Looking at the story from the outside many centuries later, Abigail's action may not seem surprising, but for her, living with a financially successful husband who organised scores of servants, it may have felt most unnatural to act against his wishes. She lived under a very strong tradition of obeying and backing the whims of a husband. Yet we can conclude that she had already built a reputation for wisdom. Verse 3 says she was known as both beautiful and wise, and in verse 14 Nabal's young servant apparently realised he should come to her because she would do the best thing.

It was certainly the wisest move. She saved the lives of the many people who worked for Nabal and did David a favour in preserving him from the guilt of shedding human blood.

Yet the truth is that Abigail consciously, without discussion, and on her own initiative, went against the wishes of her husband. She made a decision alone concerning the family's assets and God accepted and apparently applauded her action, while condemning her husband's.

In these studies we have talked of shared decision making, but this is different. It is one person of a couple making decisions. We ask ourselves, in what circumstances can an Abigail-type action be right? Sharing of major decisions must be the norm. We learnt that when studying Abraham and Sarah. For one person to go so blatantly against the other, the need would be extreme.

But what gave Abigail the courage to act so independently? Perhaps God guided her. Perhaps she knew she had a right to judge right from wrong quite apart from her husband's wishes. Perhaps she knew she was not a child to accept orders with no thoughts of her own. Perhaps she felt accountable for her own actions in the sight of God.

Abigail also took an initiative outside her own family and private life and was praised for it, with apparent approval from God. That is different from the teaching of people who still say, in spite of the many stories in the Bible of women with a function outside the home, that a woman's place is in the home.

It certainly puts in question the 'headship' theory that a husband must always be the ruler of the home, when we see that Abigail was praised and Nabal received the ultimate punishment of death.

But there is more yet. Abigail was a woman, who by her diplomacy, saved the lives of all her family's servants and kept David and his men from the guilt of murder. Mediating, keeping open the channels of communication, conciliating, keeping the peace, are often the skills of women both in families and in society. Many women gain extended experience as the peace-makers in families.

In the Bible several women are notable for their peace-making efforts. We've already observed Deborah's claim to fame after the initial battle which was followed by forty years of peace and prosperity. The wife of Pontius Pilate tried to persuade him not to sentence Jesus, this just man, to death. But the most spectacular success was that of Esther. By her diplomatic moves, fragile as walking on eggshells, she persuaded the king of Persia to save the lives of thousands of Jews who were to be slaughtered.

Perhaps in a large number of couples the wife is the natural and more skilled diplomat. If she is, she should use her skills both inside the home and out in society.

9

Marriages at the Struggling Edge

Some Bible marriages with mistakes to avoid

We have seen the human struggles of Abraham and Sarah, Eve and Adam, Isaac and Rebekah, Abigail and Naboth. We have examined the positive models in Deborah and Lappidoth, Manoah and his wife, and will see more in the Shunnamite couple, Huldah and Shallum, Zechariah and Elizabeth, Mary and Joseph.

We can also learn from marriages depicted in the Bible that serve as warnings of what not to do. Some made a bad start and continued the same way. One started as a royal affair, moved through manslaughter and then, because of a repentant heart, finished as a loving and caring marriage.

Job and his wife

One of the oldest books of the Bible tells the story of Job with little about his wife, but that small piece (Job 2:9) has a lesson.

Job and his family enjoyed enormous wealth, not in a bank balance but, as was normal then, in livestock – several thousand sheep, three thousand camels, five hundred pairs of oxen, five hundred donkeys and many servants. They could be proud of their family of seven sons and three daughters. But Job, remaining always humble, sacrificed regularly to God for himself and for his family.

When God allowed rustlers to remove the stock, allowed a firebolt, and allowed the sons and daughters, feasting in the home of one of the brothers, to be destroyed by a cyclonic wind which lifted the roof and dropped it on them, Job submitted to God and worshipped. When Satan inflicted disgusting sores from the top of his head to the sole of his foot, Job sat, miserable, among the ashes of the fire.

Here was his wife's chance to support her husband in the terrible calamity, or for the couple to support each other, to weep together and to keep honouring God, but she not only failed, she hurt him badly.

'Do you still persist in your integrity?' she asked. 'Curse God and die.'

She must have been in shock herself. She felt the loss as much as Job. But she did not determine to hold on to God, acknowledging their lives and the circumstances were not out of control. Her question really was, 'What's the use of living? Why don't we give up and die?' And, worse, she criticised Job for keeping his honest relationship to God and continuing his trust in God and others.

Her reaction was no help at all to Job. He would cling to God Almighty. And her attitude was so opposed to his own feelings that he could not respect her. 'You speak like any foolish woman would speak,' he accused. 'Shall we receive the good at the hand of God and not receive the bad?' He could see the broader perspective. God had in the past given everything they could possibly want, but all was a gift then, and all would ever be a gift that was not their right. They could not complain when it was gone. Job spoke very cuttingly to his wife. She may indeed have dragged him further into depression, but he classified her as brainless.

Their stresses were enormous. Not surprisingly Job and his wife bickered. Perhaps the lesson for us is that husbands and wives need to both keep trusting the power and control of God in the universe and in their lives. Perhaps we can weep with those who weep, but not despair with those who despair.

Elkanah, Peninnah and Hannah

The story about the parents of the prophet Samuel, told in 1 Samuel 1 and 2, starts with a God-fearing trio, regular in their costly yearly offerings at the national shrine at Shiloh. Elkanah used to travel up to Shiloh, bringing his whole family – Peninnah with her sons and daughters, and Hannah who was childless.

The trouble in the family started every time he gave out the portions of the sacrificed roast lamb to Peninnah and her children, and a double portion to Hannah, just because he loved her more than Peninnah, even though she was barren. And Peninnah used to needle Hannah.

'You're a failure,' she would harass. 'You're no use to Elkanah if you don't have children. He might be soft enough to give you extra mutton, but what good are you?'

Hannah felt bad enough already without such words heaped on her. Even today in the societies where the chief task of women is to produce the next generation, life for a barren woman hardly seems worth living. Peninnah had plenty of reason for feeling provoked. She knew Elkanah favoured Hannah with more of the sacrificial offering because he loved her more.

As for Elkanah, he was, by his position as the man in a patriarchal family and therefore the boss, the one who should sort out the problem between Peninnah and Hannah. However, he not only weakly did not try, but he made it worse by his favouritism.

Peninnah, annoyed that Elkanah loved Hannah more than her, and proud she had children, manipulated for position by putting Hannah down. Hannah didn't shout back or retaliate. Perhaps she was very sweet natured. She was certainly devout and a woman of prayer. Yet powerless. She could not change her situation nor Peninnah's treatment of her. Neither, apparently, did she complain to Elkanah.

And Elkanah himself does not appear to practise mutual respect and understanding in marriage. He was so sure of his own importance that he did not even realise how unhappy Hannah was – Hannah whom he thought he loved so much. He had not even given her his attention enough to know how sad she felt deep down that she had no children, nor to find out how much Peninnah riled her.

'Why do you weep?' he asked, a man full of himself. He thought **he** would be more important to her than ten sons. How could he think that when he so seriously lacked closeness to her? His position of power, handing down favours to whomever he wished, blinded him to his own insensitivity.

And this was at the very time when he thought he acted lovingly to Hannah. He was merely sentimental. That was the result of power lying in the hands of one partner in the marriage.

In Elkanah both the marriage of convenience to Peninnah with its children, and the marriage of love to Hannah with its sentiment, were inadequate. He did not relate well or deeply to either. Neither relationship allowed a man and woman a mutual meeting of minds with mutual respect and considerate understanding each of the other's needs and concerns.

Despite the fact that Elkanah thought he loved Hannah, he was only intimate with each in a physical way. With neither was he mentally or emotionally intimate. And neither woman was able to criticise him or tell him his short-comings because he had full power over them. They could not even point it out if they thought a decision was inappropriate or unfair.

But during the story Hannah gained more strength. She decided, on her own initiative, not even taking Elkanah into her confidence, to pray for a child. She presented herself before the Lord at the temple deeply distressed, praying and weeping bitterly. She vowed, 'O Lord of hosts, if only you will look on the misery of your servant, and remember me, and not forget your servant, but will give to your servant a male child, then I will set him before you as a Nazirite until the day of his death.'

A vow was highly significant, so important that women were not considered responsible enough to make a vow and take its consequences. A little earlier the Bible (Numbers) allows for a husband to nullify a wife's vows when he hears them. But if her husband says nothing to her about her vows then he validates them.

A ruling like this worked against single party decisions in marriage, especially against such decisions by the wife. A husband was required by this rule to consider a vow made by his wife and decide whether to give his assent or not. If he accepted it at the time, he was not permitted later to change his mind. The inappropriateness of a single individual making a binding vow is shown in some other Bible stories such as the one about Jephthah, one of the judges, who vowed he would sacrifice whoever came first to his door when he came home victorious from battle. His only child, a daughter came out dancing. He should never have made the vow, and he should have broken it because her life was more valuable than his words. If Jephthah had discussed the foolish vow with his wife, he would probably have never made it.

In the story of Hannah, Elkanah totally accepted her vow that she would bring up the child as a Nazirite with no strong drink and never a haircut.

Meanwhile elderly Eli, the priest, thought Hannah had been drinking because her lips moved but no sound came, so she explained that she was praying from great anxiety and vexation. He blessed her with a prayer for her peace and she went back to their lodgings with a heart so much lighter that her face did not even look sad.

The proof of Hannah's prayer lay with what followed. When they went home, she became pregnant and later gave birth to baby Samuel. And because Hannah had gained new confidence since her assertive prayer and promise, she grew very clear-headed about what would be best for Samuel. She made the suggestion to Elkanah that she should not go to Shiloh the next year, though it was not even outside the territory of the tribe of Ephraim, and he concurred with her plan, making it their joint decision. He said, 'Do what seems best to you. Wait until you have weaned him: only, may the Lord establish his word.'

Perhaps something had changed there. It's only a hint, but maybe Elkanah and Hannah had a better system now of discussing things together and deciding together.

When Samuel was old enough to go to live at the temple, Hannah took him and personally sacrificed a bull for Samuel's dedication to the service of God saying he was 'lent to the Lord for as long as he lives'. Each year Hannah made Samuel linen clothes for his formal rituals and took them when they went to sacrifice, and Eli the priest blessed Elkanah and Hannah asking God to reward them with children for their gift of Samuel to the shrine. That blessing worked too. Hannah later had three sons and two daughters.

For us looking at the story now, we find Hannah and Elkanah came out the other side of that experience with a greater understanding of two things – the power of desperate prayer, and a bigger view of who Hannah was as a person.

Hannah was not just a figure for Elkanah to dote on in a sentimental way, but a woman with strong feelings, strong prayers and strong opinions. Elkanah needed to learn that, but so did Hannah herself. She needed to find out that she could take initiatives. She could determine that Samuel would be a Nazirite, and she could decide when he would start serving at the temple.

And Elkanah learnt that Hannah was worth understanding and listening to as well as loving.

Ahab and Jezebel

The first time we meet Ahab and Jezebel in 1 Kings 16:29 they are working on evil plans. In fact you could say the only good thing about this couple was their unity. They never seem to have the slightest difference of opinion. The warning for us as readers will be that it is possible to have an equal and sharing marriage which is powered by evil. Unless a marriage is powered by the Maker of the universe, and run on principles of right, justice and goodness, it can go deep into destruction.

King Ahab had already chosen to do evil when he married Jezebel the daughter of the king of Sidon and worshipped the foreign god Baal with her. Ahab built a temple and altar to Baal in his major city, Samaria, and also an asherah, a sacred pole for worshipping Canaanite gods. Things went downhill in a very short time, and soon, the people made child sacrifices to mark the rebuilding of Jericho.

Next comes the story of Elijah and the contest at Mount Carmel. Jezebel had already killed many of the prophets of the Almighty when, during a time of drought and famine, God told Elijah (1 Kings 18:1) to let Ahab know it would rain soon. At Mount Carmel in front of hundreds of Israelites, the prophets of Baal failed to bring fire down on the sacrifice but God answered Elijah's prayer for fire and later for rain. When Ahab told Jezebel what had happened, she was furious and immediately sent a message to Elijah saying, 'May the gods deal with me, be it ever so severely, if you're not as dead as one of the prophets of Baal by this time tomorrow.'

She sounded vicious. Elijah fled.

The story moves next to a difference between Ahab and Ben-Hadad the king of Aram who marched up, surrounded Ahab's city, Samaria, and besieged it. With bold assertions he claimed all Ahab's silver and gold and fairest wives and children. Ahab, scared, promised everything.

But Ben-Hadad raised his stakes and demanded to search the palace as well. Ahab and his men stood their ground and then attacked, successfully, with God's help. However they let Ben-Hadad go and made a treaty with him. This was not what God wanted, so a prophet let Ahab know he would lose his own life because he'd not fully carried out God's commission.

The story moves away from battlefields. Jezebel features again. Ahab was unhappy, sulking in bed because he wanted to buy a nearby vineyard for a vegetable garden near his palace, but the owner, Naboth, would not sell. Jezebel reckoned she knew what to do to keep her husband happy. Reminding him that he was, after all, the king, she told him to get up, eat some food and cheer up. She would get him the vineyard. She wrote letters, sealed them with the king's seal, and sent them to the elders and nobles of the city ordering them to set up a feast where Naboth would be framed by two paid informants who would say he had cursed God and the king.

The trick worked. The city leaders believed the fabricated charge, took Naboth out past the city wall, stoned him to death and sent a message to Jezebel. Delighted, Ahab got ready to go out and claim his new vineyard, but God, represented by Elijah, intervened.

'Thus says the Lord: Have you killed, and also taken possession?' he said. 'Thus says the Lord: In the place where dogs licked up the blood of Naboth, dogs will lick up your blood.'

Elijah explained that God would bring disaster on Ahab and his household. Every male would be killed in such shocking circumstances that if they died in the city they would be eaten by dogs, and if they died in the country they would be eaten by vultures.

There was a special prophecy for Jezebel. 'The dogs shall eat Jezebel inside the city of Jezreel.' In fact the historian confirms the couple's unity in evil: 'Indeed, there was no one like Ahab, who sold himself to do what was evil in the sight of the Lord, urged on by his wife Jezebel.'

At this stage Ahab repented so completely that God gave him a reprieve so that disaster would not come till his son was king. When later Ahab died in his chariot in a battle, he was in disguise, but a chance arrow caught him between the scale armour and the breastplate. The gory details followed. The chariot was returned to Samaria where men buried the king and washed the chariot by the pool and dogs licked up his blood.

This evil couple would be united in the styles of their violent and dishonourable deaths. Soon it was Jezebel's turn. She had heard that the new king, Jehu was coming to Jezreel. She painted her eyes, adorned her head, and looking out of the window, she called down to Jehu that he'd murdered Ahab. At Jehu's instruction, three of her own servants threw her down so that her blood spattered on the wall and on the horses which trampled on her.

There's a poignancy about Jehu's words as he went into the palace. 'See to that cursed woman and bury her; for she is a king's daughter.' Jezebel was from a royal line. She could have been a noble in the full sense of the word. But she did not even get the honour Jehu intended in ordering for her to be buried. When the men went out to obey the instructions, they found nothing left by the dogs but the most gruesome remains.

And that was the revolting story of Ahab and Jezebel who abused their unity till they destroyed both themselves and their household.

Pontius Pilate and his wife

We have just a tiny snippet about Pilate's wife in Matthew 27:19. When Jesus was on trial, Pilate as the Roman representative was struggling to reach some kind of acceptable decision when along came a message from his wife. Probably it was an unusual action for her. Perhaps it took a lot of courage. Perhaps she knew it was totally out of order for her to attempt to influence the passage of justice. We can imagine she had heard about this preacher and worker of miracles and knew he had been brought to the court. We do know that she was bold enough to speak up with her important words, 'Have nothing to do with that innocent man, for today I have suffered a great deal because of a dream about him.'

You have to admire her. The Roman court was none of her business and Pilate was not known for kindness. But this Roman woman spoke up for justice for an innocent man. Her husband Pilate could have listened to her. He had the option to heed her warning and free Jesus. How different history could have been. Pilate will bear the responsibility for signing the death warrant of the Son of God for the ages to come.

A wife attempted to work for good, even though she failed to convince her husband. It is a role that wives sometimes become skilled at. A second opinion. A view from a different angle. An acute question, a warning, or a challenge. Husbands and wives both need a partner who will question actions and make sure they're taking the best way forward.

David and Bathsheba

This is the story that started as an affair and ended as a loving marriage. What we want to look at is the accountability, and what could have been done differently.

King David must have approached middle-age by the time of this story, no longer with the energy to be off fighting the battle. Perhaps he wanted to prove he had not lost his vigour in other ways. When he walked on his roof top late one afternoon and saw Bathsheba bathing, she may have been doing something that I have often seen women do in India and Nepal – stand at a water supply and, dressed in a long petticoat tied under the arms, splash water and take an all-over wash. It was not a provocative action. It was perfectly normal.

At this point David allowed himself to feel tempted and to step closer to temptation by enquiring who the woman was, and closer still by sending for her. He knew what he wanted. The situation was tricky for Bathsheba, though. We have no indication that she was anything other than happily married to Uriah. Her husband was a Hittite, not an Israelite, but he was away fighting in David's army, and exceedingly loyal to his fellow men-at-arms, as we find later. He must have been fully part of the community of Jerusalem. Bathsheba was caught between her loyalty to her husband and the need to obey the king's orders.

But perhaps she was not compelled. What options did Bathsheba have? Could she have left the room? Could she have called in a servant? Could she have said, 'David, I don't want to have sex with you. I'm a married woman. You're a married man. It would be morally wrong. And what's more, you're the king and you should set a good example. And anyway, I just don't want to do it'?

Too often people tell the story of David and Bathsheba as if Bathsheba had no other choice, as if she was a child or a plaything. But she was a grown woman and no stranger to the sexual act. She would have known what was coming and could have avoided it. David would be unlikely to rape her. She could have shouted for help. In fact the ruling in Deuteronomy 22:23,24 goes like this. 'If there is a young woman . . . and a man meets her in the town and lies with her, you shall bring both of them to the gate of that town and stone them to death, the young woman because she did not cry for help in the town and the man because he violated his neighbour's wife.'

We have to stop and think about that. Responsibility is placed on the woman for allowing an irregular sexual act to go ahead if she's in the town, within earshot of other people, and does not call for help. Bathsheba was not an innocent party. In the eyes of God and their own law, both she and David must carry responsibility for their actions. And they must both bear the blame and punishment too.

But even when Bathsheba became pregnant, David did not see the enormity of his actions against Bathsheba and Uriah and against God's laws. He was still trying to cover up and to get his own way.

Only when Nathan the prophet told a pointed fable that made him see himself in the shocking light his actions deserved, did he recognise his actions as sin, and Nathan made sure he understood that troubled times coming for his kingdom were a direct result of his adultery. But that knowledge was not until after David had added further to his sins – deception in the palace, lies and manipulation of the battle lines to cause a murder. David had much to repent of, but he did know how to repent.

He voiced his deep remorse in Psalm 51. 'Have mercy on me, O God. Blot out my transgressions. Wash me thoroughly from my iniquity and cleanse me from my sin. I know my transgressions, and my sin is ever before me. The sacrifice acceptable to God is a broken spirit.'

God accepted David's repentance. We do not have on record whether Bathsheba experienced shame for sin or repentance for her actions. She did have to go through the death of her husband and must have felt some serious blows to her conscience in that her action in not trying to stop the adultery meant the death of an innocent man who had been loyal to her.

When Uriah was dead and Bathsheba had completed her set days of mourning, and David sent for her and brought her into his house as his wife, the story starts to look up, but not for long. Punishment must follow. The son born to David and Bathsheba became ill and died.

We see a better side of David then. Not a middle-aged philanderer, but a man deeply cut and grieved at his baby's illness, fasting, lying on the floor and pleading with God to heal the little boy. A man who also accepted God's over-ruling when the child finally died, and who then washed and dressed and went to worship the Giver of Life.

Bathsheba grieved too. And here we see that David treats Bathsheba now more as a person and not just a woman to lust for. In her distress he comforted her and helped her to heal the hurt they both felt at the loss of their son. Then, together, forgiven, suffering, and beginning again, they started another new life to nurture as caring parents. This was the child who would become Solomon the wise, the king, and the pride of both his parents.

There are gleanings here for us as readers. We can learn that God expects both men and women to be responsible in their sexual morals. There is no cop out for one or the other. There are also punishments for sin. But the beautifully healing lesson is that when a man or a woman has failed their marriage, has failed to keep God's rules of sexual purity, there is still the option of repenting and asking God to forgive. And the healing may not stop there. Many years of new life and happiness may follow as they did for David and Bathsheba after the birth of Solomon.

10

A Child Has Two Parents

Chris and Jocelyn Grantham

'Not okay for me,' thought Chris Grantham as he looked in the room for mothers who were at the hospital to care for their children. 'Oh, well, I must sleep at the hospital somehow to be with Mark. I'll try this bed in the corridor, even though it's by the women's loos. There doesn't seem to be anything else.'

While Jocelyn stayed at home to nurse 2-month-old Rachel, Chris had done the obvious thing and come to the hospital with 2-year-old Mark while he had a hernia operation.

'Hey, what do you think you're doing here, Mr Grantham?' demanded the ward supervisor when she found him an hour later. 'You can't sleep here. It looks bad having people lying round in the corridors.'

'Okay, where shall I go then? I presume the mothers don't want me in the same room as them.'

'You could sleep at home.'

Chris knew he could not do that. Mark's severe cerebral palsy (probably a result of lack of oxygen to the brain in the last two weeks before birth) left him with no control over his legs and only the tiniest response in his arms. He needed more care than the busy staff could give. But the hospital system nearly got the better of this dad. All Chris could do was go home and get a mattress for his station wagon car and bring it back to park behind the nurses' home.

Caring for Mark had become part of Chris and Jocelyn's full-time routine in the two years since Mark was born. It was an enormous undertaking. He was the most difficult baby you could possibly imagine. He required many hours to feed, vomited constantly, and wailed every time a parent left the room. Caring for him was an all-absorbing occupation every hour of the day. His spasms and colic seemed never-ending.

Then with the birth of Rachel when Mark was twenty-two months old, the complications would have become laughable if they weren't so stressful. Like the time Chris tried to sleep in the hospital corridor. Like the times when, home with the two children, Jocelyn breast-fed Rachel while Mark cried on the floor, non-stop. Jocelyn could not enjoy healthy, normal Rachel as much as she wanted, she says now. Mark was forever crying. And other times when Chris brought work home to look after Rachel while Jocelyn took Mark to therapy, Rachel would cry for breast-milk and Chris could do nothing.

Fighting for survival

'We were fighting for our survival,' Chris says. 'We were totally convinced that both father and mother are responsible for care of children. We needed that, or Jocelyn would hardly have got through those days. It was bad enough with two of us on the job. They say that more than half the couples with a severely disabled child break up under the pressure, and we can believe it.'

'Mark cried much of the time, keeping us on edge day and night,' Jocelyn explains. 'And then he passed none of the physical milestones babies should pass. For months we didn't know what was wrong. Not till he was ten months old did we learn that his problem was severe cerebral palsy. Those months, and all the months after, required heavy work from both me and Chris. I spent whole days visiting hospitals, taking Mark to therapy, giving full care at home.'

'I learnt the treatments first for Mark and brought Chris in on them, so he could fully share the nursing and child care. We knew not many fathers do this but for us it was the only commonsense way. Chris walked Mark in a backpack for hours to soothe him. I'm not the care-giver. We both are. Chris takes more responsibility when he's at home. If he's away, I do it all. It's not that Chris just helps out with the odd good deed. If he did only that I wouldn't have survived.

'Once when Mark was small Chris went to a Christian retreat house for a weekend and found it so good he got me to go also for a weekend. Not many couples do that. We don't add up who has done how many tasks or how many hours or what each is due. If we did that one would live in bitterness feeling hard done by. But if an imbalance does develop, we talk. We both feel responsible for the house and the children, Chris as much as I. And it's a sacrifice. We both feel Christians are called to sacrifice at times, not just the women. The Bible asks PEOPLE to live sacrificially.'

Lifestyle change

When Mark was eighteen months and Chris was finishing his job contract with Tertiary Students' Christian Fellowship (TSCF), he was feeling the effects of the year's hard work as office administrator and felt he had no reserves left. He blew his holiday leave by working reduced hours and wondered what to do next. He laughed that he wanted a job with short hours and long holidays, not much responsibility and reasonable pay. Friends laughed with him, but incredibly he found one – teaching at the Correspondence School. That made things manageable for a while.

But in another two years Jocelyn felt over-burdened with child care, with the ordinary pressures of eighteen-month-old Rachel and the total commitment needed to look after and encourage Mark. They needed a further lifestyle change.

This time they made a conscious decision to work against the view that women should be totally responsible for care of children and sick family members. The burden was too great for one. Jocelyn had already lost some of her confidence for speaking in front of people, even though she was a trained teacher. She was too tired to think sometimes.

They decided to job share, working at the Correspondence School for enough hours to add up to one salary. Chris taught accounting and Jocelyn taught English language and literature. She needed a change and now at last she had some time off from caring for Mark. Chris cared for both Rachel and Mark when it was his turn, took Mark to therapy or stayed home with them many hours of the week.

They grinned when they told some friends they spent most of their time in the bedroom! They had two desks there and worked often from home.

'It was great, the lower pressure of living in a job share deal,' enthuses Chris. 'I think men shouldn't be denied the opportunity for pastoral work in their church or to be with their children. I thoroughly enjoyed looking after the kids. Enjoyed it more than Jocelyn did. I could have continued it for the rest of my life.'

The Granthams shared the one job for over five years, not always understood by Christian friends either. Some thought it was odd, others thought it excusable in view of Mark's needs. Others offered put-downs, probably in total ignorance of how they appeared to the couple.

'Chris's gifts are being wasted,' said one person in the church. Chris and Jocelyn thought this gave importance only to a father's abilities outside the home. What if a father has gifts in childcare? Which Chris has. And the view also ignores the possibility that a mother may have gifts to use outside the home which could be of value in a paid job or to enrich the kingdom of God.

'You're not being stretched,' said a friend. 'You're marking time.' But Chris thought, 'Well, Jocelyn has already stayed home more than four years. Shouldn't she get a chance to feel stretched instead of tired?'

'Men in part-time jobs are not successful in life,' was the impression given by others. Nobody thinks that of women who work part-time. But Chris knew it could count against him if he later wanted a full-time job.

Chris did, however, feel rather isolated. He felt ill at ease in the church women's coffee mornings. He could take the children to a woman friend and do a child swop, but once the children were at school he had no excuse to visit and there were no men to call on. He felt more cut off in the community than a woman would, but he felt quite happy. There was plenty to do to keep him well occupied and learning.

Later the Granthams did change to Chris as bread-winner again. He took the opportunity to return to TSCF as General Secretary, while Jocelyn did voluntary work in the church and community around it. They had to think hard about that too. Occasionally she had an important appointment to keep or community class to teach when one of the children was sick, and needed care at home. They decided that her work was important, whether it was paid or not. Sometimes Chris took time off his paid work to fulfil a home need when Jocelyn was not available. Either might relinquish a right on an occasion to fill a need. Jocelyn felt a deep satisfaction as she initiated and ran the Karori Wellness Centre for helping people in their part of the city.

'How does equal decision making really work out?' people asked. 'Surely one person has to make the final decision. You can only have one boss.' The answer for the Granthams is to let whoever is more informed on a topic take the lead.

'Chris, trained as an accountant, does the finances, though I make a point of knowing where our finances are,' Jocelyn elaborates. 'We don't often disagree, but if we do, we defer to the one with more information. When there's something important to plan, like a loan or an investment or buying a car, we discuss it first. We had a joint cheque account at the start, but some years ago we chose separate accounts, partly so we had discretionary funds for something as simple as birthday presents. Anyway our styles are quite different. I'm easy going about recording purchases, but Chris would breathe down my neck wanting me to copy his own meticulous detail. We had to learn to stand back and allow each other to do things our own way.'

Moving to Auckland

'For major decisions, like a job change that requires shifting house, we must both feel totally sure. When Chris received an invitation to direct the home end of a mission, Interserve, in Auckland, 600 kilometres from where we lived in Wellington, we needed to talk in great depth, especially because of Mark's needs.

'The only prompt to moving was that Chris's job contract was ending. Everything else was fine in Wellington, especially the supports for looking after Mark, the Wellness Centre, my teaching job, friends, the satisfying work in the church. I was not keen to leave. Chris was interested in the position but it required travel, and he did not push it. He thought we wouldn't move. I couldn't feel happy with any positive moves towards it. He delayed giving an answer. He wouldn't take the job if I was not happy, and I simply couldn't hurry my feelings.

'Just at this stage Chris's aunt paid for us to visit her in England and we took a holiday overseas. That disruption from my normal routine gave me a distance view and started the separation from the community work I had built up. If Chris had put the pressure on, I'd perhaps have moved, resentfully, but, because he gave me time, and God made the provisions, I eventually felt fine about it. I felt the wrench of leaving, but it was a time for change.

'And then God gave a bonus in the shape of a very good part-time, then full-time, teaching job for me as well at a good private school. That was important as we decided to have a house built which would suit our wish to entertain, and the needs of Mark, by then fifteen years old, who will obviously be with us for many years yet. He has an electric wheelchair requiring easy access and also needs hoists and plenty of space. We don't know whether it's faith or madness, but our mortgage means I must work as well as Chris.

'I feel grateful to God for this job. He had a niche for me that gave me the chance to contribute to people outside our family and contribute my finance towards our family as well. Now I've had the satisfaction of setting up an English learning centre for new immigrant students.'

Two parents for the teenagers too

Now that both husband and wife work full-time, instead of part-time, how do they organise their household? The main thing is it fits people's time and needs, they find. Caring for Mark still takes hours in the day. Chris is a morning person so he does daily the first 45 minutes of toilet, shower, dressing, and Jocelyn takes over the next 30 minutes of breakfast and packed lunch to have him ready for the pick-up bus at 7.30a.m. for the special unit at a government day school.

After school he can enter the house by using his electronic device to open the door, but someone must empty the toilet bag, get him a snack, take him out for something to do. He really needs teenage company but so often there are only parents to be company for him. And on top of that, like anyone else, he has periods of illness, but with him the extra care is anything but mild. Sometimes he'll vomit several times a day and his parents must keep on cleaning up. Or, if he has diarrhoea, do two or three extra changes a day and a shower as well. He certainly needs two parents.

By both pulling their weight, Chris and Jocelyn can make a contribution to God's kingdom from their home. Sometimes if Mark is ill or needs to go for therapy, Chris has to take time from work and make it up at the weekend. Sometimes he works at home to be available. And the parents continue the entertaining at home. For years it was students and church people. Now it's often also committees.

'We enjoy hospitality and see it as important,' Chris comments. 'We complement each other, and can do a reasonable amount because we share. Jocelyn usually cooks and I organise drinks, clearing, dishes, and both do talking. We don't even discuss the tasks. We just do them. We have lots of evenings when, after the people have gone, one of us will say, "Now, that was really good." '

'Chris has gifts for his work quite apart from his administration,' Jocelyn adds. 'He's got a personal flair for jokes and fun times. The students used to love it. It's now lots of fun to entertain the missionaries and candidates whom we invite round.'

I found it myself when we drank coffee at their place. While my daughter was surprised to get only five sips of coffee because her mug had a false floor, I got the mug with a little hole that let me think I'd carelessly spilt as I drank. We roared with laughter.

But there's another area I want to ask Jocelyn and Chris about. Their goal in parenting. I've seen in Mark an extraordinarily outgoing teenager, volunteering to speak in church when his speech is so slurred it is hard to understand, going abseiling at scout camps, and raising money for his three sponsored World Vision children in India, Colombia and Africa by selling chocolates from his wheelchair in shopping malls. What did they do to build such character into their son?

'We have a philosophy that he should be as independent as possible,' Jocelyn explains. 'We'd rather he was abseiling on the end of a rope than sitting rocking in a corner. We do put in a lot of effort. We go to all lengths to support his collecting for World Vision. Chris helps him set up in a shopping mall and then goes and works with his laptop computer in the van or reads, from 10.00a.m. to 2.00p.m., accepting he'll get very little else done on Saturday, and not frustrated that this leaves him little time for personal interests.

'We did lots of fun things with the children when they were small,' she adds. 'Things like making up mystery stories where Mark could take a major role. We started with the childhood "Golden Books". Then someone gave us a video camera and Chris and the children made their own videos of *Knight Rider*, or *Chariots of Fire* with the wheelchair on the beach. Mark and Rachel both got a lot from it and Mark found hours of enjoyment from later watching them.

'There are few things they can do together, so Rachel has her own interests. She's caring and artistic, loves making little gifts for friends, and delights in her ballet lessons.

'We can't do many of the things other families do for holidays. We can't even go for an evening walk for more than ten minutes. Mark likes company. If we do make a trip without him, Chris videos something of it so he can share the experience. In school holidays Chris takes Mark every time he goes shopping, even though it's an effort with the wheelchair, and takes him swimming – lifting, changing, carrying, laughing.'

One sees Chris's zany streak as a father just by looking in Mark's bedroom. Fake frogs decorate the room and a mock arm hangs out of a drawer. Chris has looked for ways to make him laugh. Jocelyn is often the chauffeur taking Rachel to music or dancing lessons, with many hours taking Mark to physiotherapy, to specialists, responding to needs. She brings and takes friends for Mark. She's so sure he needs young company.

Jocelyn and Chris seem to be doing a remarkable job, taking their parenting so seriously, or should I say hilariously.

In the Bible story of the Shunammite couple in 2 Kings 4:8-37, I find a forerunner of Jocelyn and Chris's hospitality, their shared initiating of family plans, and their care for a son when he was sick.

The Shunammite couple

In the subsistence farming society of old Israel, hospitality to the traveller was a virtue. It is still like that in the hills of a country like Nepal. I benefited from the custom myself the time I arrived with my daughter, exhausted after an eleven hour day of trekking, at a village with no lodging house.

We do not know the names of this couple at Shunem, but the Bible describes the wife as wealthy. The wealth may have come from the husband, who was much older than she was, but the fact that it is mentioned in connection with the wife gives the impression that the wealth belonged to her. Perhaps she held property in her own right and was in the habit of making decisions accordingly. Certainly she made household decisions when it came to harbouring a traveller and later managing the outdoor servant. Probably her invitation to Elisha and his servant, Gehazi, to stop and eat a meal was specifically because he was a prophet.

We realise the good level of communication between her and her husband as she suggested Elisha, who passed regularly, must be a holy man and they could make a small roof chamber with a bed, table, chair and lamp, for him to stay in whenever he came to them. She initiated the idea, and they must have liked working together to carry it out, for in a short time we find Elisha, on his next visit, comfortably ensconced in the little room wondering with Gehazi how he can say thank you.

They called her up to ask what she'd like as a thank-you gift. But she was not greedy, nor ambitious for herself, just pleased to help. She did not want a word spoken on her behalf to the king or the army general either.

'I live among my own people,' she said.

Now Elisha and Gehazi racked their brains. 'What can we do for her, then?'

'What about the fact she has no son and her husband is old?'

'The very thing. Call her up again.' She stood at the door and Elijah told her, 'This season next year, all in good time, you'll be cuddling a baby boy in your arms.'

'No, don't say that. Don't tease me, man of God,' she exclaimed. But it was no teasing, for she became pregnant and had a son just as he'd said. And the thing we notice as we analyse the relationships in the household of this couple is that the visitors deal with the wife. She seems to be the leader of the team, or the one to deal with exclusively on matters of relating to strangers, hospitality, home extensions, thank-yous, even additions to the family. And there is no suggestion anyone thought this improper, or that she was not allowing her husband to be head of the household. We conclude they ran it jointly.

In fact Elisha and Gehazi conversed readily with the woman more than the man in a healthy and warm relationship. Perhaps she was an outgoing person who, with a husband who trusted her, spoke for both of them. Perhaps the trust between them enabled the wife to take a major decision later in an emergency over their son's health.

Action in an emergency

The next part of the story happened some years later in a situation which is still all too common in Third World countries where people depend only on the resources they can grow in their own valley. In isolated rural areas still up to four in ten children die before the age of 5 years.

In this story in Shunem the precious young son went out to the harvest field one day with his father, trotting behind the reapers with their sweeping scythes. Was it sunstroke, or something more sinister? Suddenly, he complained to his father, 'My head, my head.'

Promptly the father got a servant to carry the boy home to his mother, but the damage was already done. He sat on her lap and died at noon.

However, the woman would not give up so easily. It was time for action. She placed the limp little body upstairs on Elisha's bed and hurried down to give some instructions.

'Send one of the servants and a donkey,' she called to her husband. I'll go and get the man of God.'

'But, but it's not a feast day or a Sabbath. Why do you want to see him?'

'It'll be all right,' she called back as she threw the saddle on the donkey and instructed the servant, 'Give it all you've got, man. Don't wait round for me.'

She would not even talk to Gehazi when Elisha sent him to meet her. She grabbed Elisha's feet, sobbing so hysterically that Gehazi wanted to push her away. Finally she got her plea out. 'Did I ask you for a son? Didn't I say, "Don't mislead me"?'

Even though Elisha sent Gehazi hurrying to lay his special staff on the form of the boy, the mother vowed she would never go home again unless he came too. Her insistence succeeded. Elisha returned with her, went upstairs to the dead child, lay on him, warmed him, and brought him back to life. When Gehazi called her she bowed to Elisha in deepest gratitude, picked up her son and scurried downstairs from that sacred room.

And as we consider the story we notice it was the wife with her great hospitality who took the initiatives, inviting Elisha in to eat and suggesting the rooftop visitor's room. Although she was wealthy and accustomed to giving orders to servants, she remained humble at heart when offered the chance to make a request to the king.

We see that she and her husband acted together in their welcome to the prophet. He trusted her to do what was right in the emergency, not even going along to protect her on the road, because she knew she had a task that she personally would perform. We see the independence that ran beside their joint decisions when she resolutely went off to find Elisha, and assertively insisted he return to the house with her. And when we reach verse 37 we find she had not omitted the virtue of gratitude. She fell at Elijah's feet bowing to the ground in her thankfulness.

What a couple to learn from, and how strong and independent their partnership. God seemed to like them that way, and bless them for their initiatives and their strength.

11

We're Still Learning

John and Janette Fawcett

I first met John Fawcett at work where he used to call in regularly, a smiley man with greying hair and beard making him look older than he really is. It was some months before I realised he and his wife were doing something very considered in their marriage. When I asked if I could interview him and Janette, he said, 'Yes, sure, but we're still learning, you know. We still don't always get it right.'

'That's fine by me,' I replied. 'We need people who'll be honest. We don't need to think that an equal marriage is only achieved by people on a pedestal who never make mistakes. We'll learn from you.'

So one Tuesday evening I drove out to their house and found John and Janette working on the sitting room floor. He was packing newsletters into envelopes for something he was doing for his part-time work, and Janette had beside her a stack of marking from school. She put it aside while we talked. A fire hissed in the grate as I settled myself in an easy chair by Janette and learnt that she taught science at a large and highly regarded girls' school.

'Well, how did you two meet?' I asked.

'We were at university in Dunedin in the South Island,' they told me. 'We shared in youth work at our church. We were colleagues on a committee then and at an early stage we wanted our marriage to be just as equal. While we were engaged we did a series of Bible studies together on mutual marriage.'

'My parents were strong-minded people who both worked outside the home when I was an adolescent,' John elaborates. 'I was the oldest and took my turn to cook and clean and wax the floor. My parents had an equal marriage. My scientist father believed in justice for less privileged people and got us thinking about equality long before we married.

'Our family used to have what we called "free and frank discussion" that sometimes ran for three hours. It could be heated but there was no animosity – more like a student lounge conflict of ideas, not conflict of people. But some people thought we'd had a major family row.'

Janette's family was totally different.

'My father felt it was his task to rule the family,' she explains. 'He wasn't always a hard man, but I think life was very difficult for my mother at times. When I was a teenager, I had to fight for permission every time I wanted to go out. When I became a convinced Christian, I expected to think for myself, and that's why I went all the way to Dunedin to go to university. It was far enough away from home to let me be free.'

They feel now they were a little young, but John and Janette married when they were twenty and twenty-two, and, though they tried right from the start to make everything equal in their marriage, they say it didn't always work out. Janette found she still expected John to make the main decisions – a result, she thinks of the teaching she had most often received from other Christians.

John tells a story about buying a car.

'We'd both contributed finances to buying a good car but then I wanted to buy a van. I fantasised about the two of us on getaway holidays, tripping around the South Island, sleeping in our own van. I didn't ask Janette's opinion – she was unhappy with the plan, but didn't speak up.

'I bought the van. But we never did use it for camping holidays. We lost $1000 on it when we sold it and that was serious for unwaged students.

'The trouble came from not discussing our feelings about decisions. We thought logic more important. We had some money, we thought we needed the van, and the van appeared to suit. We didn't allow a step where one person could say, "I don't feel good about this." Probably Janette mentally accused me of stuffing up the whole thing.

'But at least we learnt. Later decisions, like not having children at the start, travelling overseas, saving money for a house, we made with both feeling and logic.'

All for a job

But they still have a story of a time some years later when they did not get it right and the mistake nearly broke their marriage. By this stage, living in Christchurch, still in the South Island, they had Matthew aged twenty-one months and Christine three months. John was well into a career, although he still had two years of service to repay the government department that had financed part of his university work.

He was offered a job which would be a major career step in the North Island in Wellington. Janette did say that she did not like Wellington and her friends were in Christchurch not Wellington, and anyway there was still the two-year bond to fulfill, but John had some quick answer. He really wanted that job.

He accepted the offer and resigned from his job. They put their house on the market, found buyers, signed up, accepted the deposit, and friends fixed the date of their farewell party. But things at home were getting worse.

'It was like an emotional wall between us,' Janette says. 'Everything about the job and the shift looked logical, and we'd prayed and things seemed to be working out, but I was sitting at home stewing. I didn't think it was right, and the closer we got to the time, the less I wanted to go. John knew I was unhappy, but I hadn't said why. I was concerned about the bond, that we might have to pay back $18,000 or two years salary.

'Suddenly one day I was sure. I phoned John at work and said, "I'm not going to Wellington." '

That did it for John. He saw no future in placing his profession ahead of his marriage. He phoned the Wellington employer and said he was not coming. He had not actually signed a written contract, so this was not considered too serious. But they'd sold their house. They phoned the couple who had bought it, asking 'Can we buy our house back, please?' They agreed to pay legal fees and agent's fees, and, amazingly, the couple sold it back.

'As for us,' say John and Janette, 'we were too astounded at the turn of events to blame each other. We sat and prayed together. We again made the agreement that if one of us was not happy, even if there was no logical reason, then we wouldn't do it. Decisions are not such a major issue now because we have a routine of talking things out together.

'We did leave Christchurch and leave our friends there two years later. We both felt okay then. Decisions need both logic and intuition.'

John contrasts Janette's attitudes with some of the people he meets professionally as a counsellor with an MA in Social Work. He has often seen women who are damaged not physically but psychologically by fathers or husbands. These women have been taught by their upbringing or their environment that their feelings and thoughts in making a decision do not matter, and it becomes so strong they let life happen around them without bothering to have many opinions, and even less able to take part in decisions.

He finds it difficult as a counsellor at times because a high proportion of women believe a man will rescue them, he says. They think the men in their lives, or a new man, or a male counsellor, will come and solve all their problems. Christian women sometimes fail to take responsibility for themselves because they see men as better and closer to God than women.

Why bother about roles?

John and Janette took a step further in their chosen equality when they decided to do a complete swap from the traditional wife and husband roles.

'We felt excited about the change. It held more potential for us than the slots we were in before,' they claim. 'We were both ready for professional stimulation.'

Janette found the demanding full-time job as a science and chemistry teacher and co-dean of the third year students in a large grammar school. John first worked part-time as a counsellor with a medical practice and later took on the task of setting up a rapidly growing Christian network called Lovelink, among churches reaching out to the needy in their communities.

'We were surprised,' they comment, 'how few of our friends and acquaintances could understand that John was responsible for the children and running the house. People seemed to think that if Janette worked full-time and John helped with the housework, that was okay, but when we explained that Janette was the breadwinner and John the homemaker, they were uncomfortable and let us know.'

But the couple had seen other families where the wife worked full-time and remained totally responsible for running the house, even if she delegated some of the tasks to the husband. They did not think this was fair.

Preparing the meals became John's role, not merely carrying out Janette's suggestions. He planned, purchased, cooked and cleaned up. John took on all the child care and house work so Janette did not even know if the sheets on son Matthew's bed were changed, or whose house Christine was playing at after school. And that did not come easily for a mother when mothers are expected to know these details.

'The first two or three months were horrific,' Janette recalls. 'I'd sit in the lounge doing school preparation and feel I shouldn't leave preparing the meal to John along with caring for the children, so I'd go and offer to help cook the meal. We had to agree that John could ask me questions, but I must keep out of the kitchen. It was so difficult. We had to try hard, very hard, to keep to our plan.

'The difficulty was not even that John didn't know how to do the tasks. We both knew how to run a house. But the tasks were part of me. I just did them without thinking. But if I did them now I would be taking from John.'

So why did they bother? This couple had thought it through very carefully, concluding that the huge advantage of reversing the traditional husband and wife roles lay with John's skills for the local community. When he worked part-time, it suited fine to pick up little Christine from kindergarten at noon. He felt he developed some brilliant relationships with the parents who were childcarers in the community. He still has good talks with them now some years later. It was all part of his work for Jesus.

The people they knew best understood the couple, especially their closest friends from church. At a church home group they would joke about them in a pleasant way for their reversed roles, for they could see their desire to serve the community. But they did find their casual acquaintances were confused about their family organisation. Women would phone asking for Janette when they wanted to invite one of the children over to play, but Janette wasn't at home, or if she had come in, might not even know where the children were. And one thing she in fact missed was the chance to be friendly with the other mothers. But she did counterbalance that with all the input into the lives of the girls she taught and the friends she made on the staff of the school.

'I had no flack from the men,' John grins. 'I think they felt envy more often. I was obviously enjoying myself. No 35 minutes on the road getting to work, able to see my kids at any hour of the day. I think some would like to copy us but don't know how to get out of their conventional roles.'

And now, since this interview, John and Janette have accepted the invitation of World Vision to work in California where John is in human resource management and Janette has a teaching job.

But it is time to stop and think about roles, conventional or otherwise, along with a Bible story. Huldah and Shallum were a Bible couple who did not live by the social roles of their time in history, yet nobody even said they were unconventional. Their story, placed in the days of King Josiah, appears twice in the Old Testament, 2 Kings 22:14–20 and 2 Chronicles 34:14–33.

Huldah and Shallum

When King Josiah of the Jews was twenty-six, the great reformer threw out from the temple the cult carvings, poles and images and the idol worship that had infiltrated the kingdom, and set about repairs to the temple of Jehovah God. Porters carried, stonemasons chipped, builders built, and when others cleared away the rubble, Hilkiah the priest found the book of the law of Jehovah written by Moses. He and Shaphan the secretary took it to Josiah.

As the words of the book were read out, Josiah tore his clothes in distress because the idol worship being practised was totally against his nation's God. He wanted to make sure the book was authoritative and what he should do next, so he sent his five counsellors to a Jerusalem prophet, Huldah the wife of Shallum, to obtain a word from God.

Huldah must already have been known as a prophet. And after this she would be seen as advisor to the king.

But immediately, if we were brought up on the 'husbands rule' model, questions spring to mind. Why did God choose Huldah as the prophet, when he could have chosen Shallum? Indeed, since she lived at the same time as Jeremiah and Zephaniah, why did not God send his message to the king through either of them?

Possibly Huldah and Shallum were a fairly young couple, if we judge by the fact that Shallum's grandfather was still alive (2 Chron. 34:22). It seems an unlikely scenario – five men in authority, acting for a sixth, a king, went to a young, probably illiterate woman (women were not taught to read), to hear God's voice. We can only suppose there had been powerful or repeated occasions when Jehovah spoke through Huldah in the past in a way that was totally recognised by people and king as the voice of God.

Huldah does her own work

By the conventions of conservative societies, men would not go to visit a woman without first asking permission from her husband, or at least letting him know. But here there seems no call for permission. Huldah relates to the king's counsellors in her own right, and gives advice for the running of the kingdom. Even today I hear radio preachers say, and read writers who claim, that a woman's sphere and expertise is the home and her husband's is outside the home. Some say a husband should be a 'covering' for his wife to relate to the outside world.

This was not Shallum's attitude to Huldah. He did not protect her from contact with business outside the home, nor even from the court of the king. That was becoming political. And indeed her reply had enormous political implications.

But there is another supposed Christian convention that this couple ignore, or never heard of. A further angle of the 'covering' theory has it that the role of a husband, is to act as a covering for his wife in her relationship to God. This way he will enable her to avoid mistakes theologically, and after all a husband represents God to a wife, the teaching says. We saw earlier (see end of chapter 2) that God requires people to relate to God themselves because they will be judged for how they acted as individuals. Here we have another clear example of a wife receiving God's word with no assistance at all from a husband, and not merely for herself or her family, but for the ruler of the country.

A powerful prophecy

However, more astounding things were to come yet from Huldah. The prophecy was no meek and mild keep-up-your-courage pep talk. It was solid politics and theology – not the run of the mill conversation of a person on the margins of decision making in society as women have often been in the past. The message for King Josiah went like this:

'Tell the man who sent you, "Yes, the Lord will destroy this city and its people. The curses will come true because my people have worshipped heathen gods and I'm angry with them. But you, King Josiah, have humbled yourself and wept before me for your people's sin. I've heard you. There's great evil coming for this city, but it won't come in your day." '

Next, without a moment's hesitation because the prophecy had come from a woman, everyone took Huldah's words with intense seriousness. We do not know why they did. Perhaps the Holy Spirit made sure the five listeners felt convinced in their hearts that this was truly God's word for the kingdom. King Josiah summoned to the temple in Jerusalem all the elders of the nation, all the priests, all the Levites, all the people, big or small. There he read the scroll out loud, or had a scribe read out, the covenant of God that was found in the temple.

Then King Josiah made a solemn promise to Jehovah God to follow the commandments with all his heart and soul and to do what was written in the scroll. He told everybody in Jerusalem and the countryside around to agree to this pact with God, and they did. The result was that Josiah got rid of all the idols and for all the rest of his life convinced the Jews to worship only Jehovah.

This is a powerful story. A young married woman was the one person God chose to receive and pass on the message that was so essential to the direction of the nation of Jews that it changed the shape of the kingdom for decades to come.

A prophet, if that person is accepted as a prophet, must by definition be a person with authority, because a prophecy has the authority of coming from God. People saw Huldah as a person of authority.

Encouraging another's gift

We wonder what Shallum and Huldah said as they talked. Huldah does not seem to be held back by Shallum from exercising her gift. Her past prophecies told the king's counsellors they could look to her for an authoritative word.

We suppose husband Shallum encouraged Huldah to speak and act with the authority that God gave her. The thought of him stepping in as the prime authority of the household to tell Huldah what to do as she related to God, to the five visitors, or gave a political forecast to the king, is far from the actual story.

And God graciously saw fit to confirm Huldah's authority by carrying out what she said would happen. May we all, women and men, encourage each other to develop and use the gifts God gives us as effectively as Huldah did.

12

Heads He Wins, Tails She Loses

The theory of headship

One sunny lunchtime Tania and I munched our sandwiches in the garden patch outside the office.

'How do you manage for looking after your children when you leave for work?' I asked, knowing she starts work at 7.30a.m. after a half-hour drive.

'Oh, my husband takes the children to kindergarten and then looks after them in the afternoon. Robert's hours are 5.30p.m. till about 2.00a.m.'

'Wow, that must take some organisation.'

'Yes, we planned it carefully when he took that job, and he won't do it for ever. But it's working out quite well in some ways. He gets plenty of time with Paul and Emma, and, by eating our evening meal early, when I come in after 4.00p.m., we enjoy good family time all together. Robert has the meal ready for us.'

'And what do you in your spare time, Beulah? Are you writing any more books?'

'Yes, I am, actually.'

'Tell me, what's this one about? Another about tuning in to God?'

'No, this is different. I'm analysing the marriages in the Bible and finding that God expected women to be responsible for their actions and not to hide behind their husbands.'

'What? You're finding that in the Bible! I'd be interested to read that. We went through a most difficult patch in our marriage when I thought everything had to revolve around Robert and I had to try to make him the boss all the time. I was reading a Christian book that said a wife shouldn't plan for herself but depend totally on her husband. I tried to, but it really messed us up. Robert said he didn't like me to be a nothing. He liked me to be able to think for myself.'

'Hey, that's interesting, Helen. Tell me about the book.'

'Well, it maintained that the Bible says a husband's role is to be the leader and make all the decisions. I tried to do it, let him be the leader and initiate every single thing in the family. But it didn't work. Robert's happier if we plan together. He wouldn't go ahead and plan something without talking to me because he would rather know whether it would suit all of us.

'I did try to do the things in the book.' Tania continued. 'But perhaps there's something wrong with me. The methods suggested either didn't feel right or just plain didn't work! If the Bible really said a woman should play sort of games of making out her husband is never wrong and he should make all decisions without asking her opinion, then Robert and I would have to go against the Bible.

'It sounds okay to say the wife should comfort him tenderly when he is discouraged, but the book said to greet him at the door when he comes from work, smiling and looking your best with the home quiet and totally organised. It's impossible with two young children eager to see Daddy. Or he comes late and I'm tired.

'Then it said to draw up a "Certificate of Leadership" and present it to him saying you will follow his leadership 100 per cent. Robert didn't even want it. And it was the biggest mistake of my life when I followed the next piece of advice – handing over to Robert all the responsibility for finances. He was lax in keeping accounts and irresponsible. I'd never again put the family through that pain of debt if it could be avoided.

'Nor will I hold back from a paid job as the book insisted wives should. My having a job is not a matter of choice. I'd prefer to be home with the children, but it would be selfish not to help out with the finances when I'm able. I don't want to put pressure on Robert to find a high powered job, or work so hard we don't see him as a family.

'At one stage in the book it said to think of something you really want and deserve and ask your husband for it in a child-like manner. I didn't do it. I hadn't anything to ask. And I'm not a child. Robert told me he married me for the thinking person I was and not to be a puppy dog.

'There was a story in the book about a couple who got back together because she totally praised her husband's every move, altered her hair and clothes to be more alluring, and left work so that he could feel manly about supporting her. It all seemed to work in the book and I desperately needed some help. But it still came down to this: It takes two to tango. If my husband didn't respond to my efforts, then he just didn't. We're past that stage now, but it wasn't the book that helped us.

'The whole thing was about being dependent, and our relationship isn't like that. I'm not dependent like a child, and Robert doesn't want me dependent. He appreciates me for myself. It sort of came between us if I was trying in an underhand way to butter him up and make him think he was the boss and that I couldn't think for myself, when really I was thinking very hard. I wasn't manipulating, but it didn't feel totally honest.

'What does work for us is when we share our thoughts and our jobs around the house. He's excellent with the children, and we're comfortable doing what we do best, which might be Robert preparing the evening meal and me managing the finances.'

I thought hard as Tania talked. Her story made me realise that practising an unthinking male headship can interrupt a couple's ability to work things out together, even their true intimacy. If a wife believes she has a role to always submit to her husband, never thinking they could acquiesce to each other's wishes on different occasions, she will not voice an opinion. Yet on thousands of occasions two heads are better than one.

If a man believes he is the boss of the home to make all the rules and all the decisions, he is not listening to his wife as a person. He assumes he knows what is best for her, and assuming dispenses with the need to discuss. Their conversation can be superficial and avoid the deepest issues. A husband and wife may then look at each other as roles that must be carried out, rather than as persons with whom to develop the deepest understanding. They cannot be really close. They lose some of their intimacy.

An unequal marriage may be very strong when a dominant partner and a submissive partner fit each other's needs for one to lead and the other to follow. But a marriage can never be healthy until both partners are fully adult.

In an unequal marriage the dominant partner does not have to be mature enough to listen to the other, whose opinion is just as valid, when the subject affects that person. And the weaker partner is treated as a child, not fully responsible for the implications of decisions made.

Christians submit first to Christ

The final authority for every Christian, in marriage as everywhere else, is Christ. That is basic, and our thinking starts from there.

By definition a Christian is a person who submits to Christ, 'Submit yourselves therefore to God.' James 4:7 And Hebrews 12:9–10 says, 'We had human parents to discipline us, and we respected them. Should we not be even more willing to be subject to the Father of spirits and live?' When things are working well, the natural outcome for a couple who submit to Christ is that, with Christ as the leader of the home, they both want to obey him, and by drawing closer to Christ draw closer to each other.

Then we take the Christian instructions further. Jesus said, 'You know that the rulers of the Gentiles lord it over them. It will not be so among you; whoever wishes to be great among you must be your servant.' Matthew 20:25-26 What Jesus taught was the opposite of all that happens in the hierarchies of his day and ours, whether in marriage or society.

Jesus condemns the 'chain of command' concept for his followers. The one kind of leadership Jesus taught and modelled was the leadership of servanthood and example. Any teaching about marriage or anything else that contradicts these high standards taught by Jesus can hardly be called 'Christian'.

If we thought a Bible command makes one person or group of Christians always less directly responsible to God, needing decisions made for them (whether because of race, sex, or economic status), we would have to look at it again, because that would be contrary to Christ's teaching.

Paul reminds his readers that Christ is our example and he took the form of a slave, giving himself sacrificially. The Bible says to give up one's rights for the sake of others, but it says it to both men and women.

All of us are priests

Evangelical Christians reject any thought of an intermediary between a person and his or her Maker. We teach that all believers have open access to the throne of God. That all believers are priests, is stated once in the book of Isaiah and six times in the New Testament, notably in 1 Peter and in Revelation.

In Old Testament times the function of priests, when only they and the prophets had direct access to God, was to act as a bridge between God and humans. This they did in three ways: by representing human beings to God with sacrifices, by mediating between one human being and another, and by teaching. 'The lips of a priest should guard knowledge, and people should seek instruction from his mouth for he is the messenger of the Lord of hosts.' Malachi 2:7

But from the New Testament on, all who believe in Christ are priests. 'You are a chosen race, a royal priesthood, a holy nation, God's own people.' 1 Peter 2:9 This has to mean they have access to God, and should carry out the tasks of priests when appropriate: to communicate between God and people, to mediate between humans, and to teach.

I grew up with the truly great teaching that there is one God and one mediator between God and human beings, Christ Jesus, himself human. 1 Timothy 2:5 But this truth, loved so much by Bible-believing Christians, is contradicted if we say a woman must have her husband over her as a 'head' who will act for her and make decisions. He would be between her and God, acting as a go-between or priest for her to her God.

The Bible view is that something that comes between a person and God has become an idol. If preachers and writers insist that a man must make decisions for his wife, they are insisting on idolatry.

In churches we may talk about the priesthood of all believers, but what appears to be practised in some churches is the priesthood of half the believers, the men. Even in these days in many churches a man leads the worship, a man prays, men take up the collection, men lead the mixed home groups and a man preaches and pronounces the benediction. Even when, as in some churches, women are welcomed to join publicly in a service, the time proportion for women may still be very low. A friend kept a record and found women had less than 15 per cent. I don't feel able to invite educated women friends to such a church. It would look to them like, 'Come and watch my men friends do their thing.'

In one church I attended the minister asked me to accept nomination to become an elder. In the congregational vote an elder needed confirmation by 75 per cent of the church. Just as the voting began, and I was the only nomination, a younger man got up and said they should not allow a woman to be an elder. The votes reached 69 per cent. Three months later another elder had resigned. There were two vacancies and still only my name put forward, and again the votes were just short of the required figure. I do not think there was anything wrong with me. I had a degree in theology, was a returned missionary, a leader among evangelical women across the city at the time. But I was a woman.

In fact the church presumably left itself very short-handed to carry out the leadership tasks. And the only conclusion I could draw, was that I was worse than nothing since it appeared worse to have my services than to have nothing.

I pondered. What do I as a woman have to do to qualify to be an elder in my church? Nothing. There was nothing I could do. I was born wrong. I would have to be born again as a male to become a leader and of equal standing with the men in the church.

But I thought I was born again already. Wasn't that enough?

I did not leave that church. I knew why they felt like that. I thought the same for decades myself. The minister even came round with some flowers, he was so disappointed at the way the voting went. And two years later, I am pleased to report, they did vote in as an elder a sweet-natured woman friend of mine.

Access to the source of wisdom

Some years before that incident of the voting, I learnt, in the difficult months after my husband Brian died, an unexpected lesson about how important it is to find the Holy Spirit as a source of wisdom. It happened like this. I was telling God as I prayed one day, 'How am I supposed to raise these four children without Brian's counsel and advice? I'm on my own, and I don't want to be.'

But the thought from John 14 stopped me in my tracks. 'And I will ask the Father, and he will give you another Counsellor, and he will be with you forever.' 'Wow,' I thought. 'That's pretty amazing. I should have known it anyway. The Holy Spirit is a lot better Counsellor than my very human husband was. He'll guide. I'll be able to get him to help me with decisions.'

If I come to Christ to ask to be redeemed, I can also receive the guidance I need to make decisions required for my life. That is true for all Christians. I mean **all** Christians. The Bible does not say a married woman has less access to the guidance of the Holy Spirit than her husband and her husband has to get all the guidance for the family. Nor does it say an unmarried woman would not be able to find God's will without a man to guide her.

All disciples, women and men, may lay claim to the promises, 'The Helper, the Holy Spirit, whom the Father will send in my name, will teach you everything,' John 14:26, and 'When the Spirit of truth comes, he will guide you into all the truth.' John 16:13

If married women should be guided always by the wisdom given their husbands, they would have no need for the Holy Spirit's presence in their lives. Or, if the Spirit indwells them, the presence could be allowed to atrophy through lack of use. But of course such a view is nonsense. John's gospel teaches that the Holy Spirit lives in Christians to guide them, all Christians, men and women, married and unmarried.

The 'head' metaphor in Paul's letters

It should be obvious, but it needs restating, that the literal meaning of head is a part of a body. When Paul uses the word head in 1 Corinthians 11 and Ephesians 5 he is using a metaphor, and we have to treat it that way.

Here is an example of another metaphor. Jesus said he was a shepherd. My father was a shepherd. I can tell you about shepherds. They look after the sheep very carefully, give them clean water and plenty of food, keep them healthy with crutching, vaccines, sheep dips for lice, tar on sores and trimming overgrown hoofs. They do all this with the goal of taking the nice warm coat off them when it suits, taking their lambs away when they are fat, and then killing the sheep itself for meat. Shepherds only look after sheep for what they can get. Is that what our shepherd, Jesus, is like?

But you tell me that is not what Jesus meant. He was not a shepherd out for what he could get. Right. The Shepherd metaphor in the Bible rests on the care of the sheep, not on how the sheep are exploited. And a metaphor may mean different things depending on the way it is used in the culture where it is written and read.

In the same way, we have to be wary as we look at the 'head' metaphor. When we move a metaphor from Greek to English, it may not have the meaning in English that it had in Greek. In fact it does not. The Greek word *cephale* is literally a head, a part of the body, but as a metaphor it means source, something like the headwaters of a stream.

In English, on the other hand, when we read head as a metaphor we think boss, authority, which is not necessarily the connotation of the Greek word head. If God intended Paul, where he used the word head, to mean boss, he could have used the Greek word *exousia*, authority.

A number of Bible commentators have in recent years pointed out this difference with careful scholarship. Readers who want to make a fuller study will want to read those books. For this chapter it may suffice to quote from some of them.

> In 1 Corinthians 11:3, 'The head of every man is Christ, the head of woman is the man, and the head of Christ is God,' the word head, *cephale*, seems to have the Greek meaning of source or origin . . . In verse 11, Paul states the essential interdependence and equality of the sexes: 'In the Lord (i.e. in their new vital relationship with Christ), woman is not independent of man, nor man of woman.' Paul as usual emphasises the new creation in Christ.
>
> People who believe that 1 Corinthians 11:3 teaches a 'chain of command' (despite the oft-repeated teachings of Christ regarding leadership as servanthood) must rearrange the verse to get the 'chain'. Paul arranged the verse as Man-Christ, Woman-Man, Christ-God. Surely if Paul wished to teach a 'chain of command' he would have used a less ambiguous word than the Greek word *cephale*, and would also have arranged it in proper order: God, Christ, Man, Woman.[1]

Often the argument for women to submit rests on Ephesians 5:21-24, 'Be subject to one another out of reverence for Christ. Wives, be subject to your husbands as you are to the Lord. For the husband is the head of the wife just as Christ is the head of the

---

1 Berkley & Alvera Mickelsen in 'Transformation' Jul/Sept 1988

church, the body of which he is the Saviour. Just as the church is subject to Christ, so also wives ought to be, in everything, to their husbands.'

First we must note that verse 21 asks us all to submit, equally. We keep this in mind while we read the next few verses which do not look like equality. We cannot say categorically that women must submit if we already know all must mutually submit.

And if the example to follow is Christ, who sacrificed himself for the church, the passage can hardly mean at the same time top-down rule. It cannot be a metaphor that makes a husband and wife into master and servant, since the husband is also required to be the servant.

> 'Thus,' comments Swartley, 'the justification for 'chains of command' that one often hears, namely, that 'when there is an impasse, someone must make the final decision' certainly cannot find support in Paul, nor in the relationship of God in Christ that is Paul's ultimate court of appeal. Such logic is supported neither by Paul's use of *cephale* nor by his view of marriage, and it is dealt a serious blow by the acknowledgment that God distributes the power of the Christian life, the Holy Spirit, to all.'[2]

The metaphor of the head has been taken much further than it goes in the Bible by churches talking about 'headship', a word that does not appear in the Bible, and 'head of the house'. Secular society also uses the label 'head of the house' in household and census surveys. Sociologists use it in the context of how many female headed households there are in an area as compared with male headed households. This assumes, without grounds, that if there is a husband then he is making the rules.

I asked my lawyer the legal meaning of the phrase 'head of the household'. Seemingly none. By law in New Zealand, and in many other Western countries, a woman is considered neither more nor less responsible than a man for what happens in a house. 'Head of the house' seems to be legally nothing more than a convenient label for filling in census forms.

---

2 *Women, Authority & the Bible,* (IVP, ed. Mickelsen, 1986, p. 92)

But the label 'head of the household' does appear once in the Bible, *oikodespotein* – literally house despot. Paul applies it in 1 Timothy 5:14 to young women! He suggests they marry, have children, and 'rule' or 'be head of' their households.

Perhaps, after all that's been said about Paul, he did think that women could, and should, rule households.

13

Looking for the Plan Ahead

A question of timing

Scene 1: Ootacamund, South India

Give us half a day off from the boarding school duties in Ootacamund in the mountains of South India, and our family is off walking. Along forest paths, past potato terraces, between tea gardens. But after nine good years we're restless. Does God want us somewhere else? Three offers of principal's positions arrive on Brian's desk. Which one? India? Nepal?

Before the rising bell one Friday morning in the girls' hostel I am supervising, I sit with a hot cup of tea.

'Deuteronomy today. Don't remember what's in this, Lord, but do let us know what you think about Nepal or India some time.

'What! Did I see that right?' I throw back the handloom bed cover and call Brian. 'Hey, listen to this. Did you know this was in the Bible? "You have been going about this hill country long enough; go north. Take your journey to the mountainous country that I will show you." '

'Wow, sure looks like Nepal!' Brian exclaims. 'There's no question that we've walked around on the Nilgiri Hills here, a lot, and Nepal certainly looks like a mountainous country to the north for us.'

We find the point rubbed in repeatedly over the next months. The position looks just right, Nepal is mentioned in several books and magazines we happen to read, letters from friends. Later when Interserve, the missionary society we join, confirms from New Zealand that they have received enough promises of support to send us onwards without returning from India, they send a telegram that unconsciously reiterates the words from Deuteronomy with a simple, 'Go north'. 'This guidance is so clear,' muses Brian. 'I wonder if God gave it so unmistakably because it's going to be tested and we have to know for sure that Nepal's the place?'

Scene 2: Pokhara Valley, West Nepal

We are here at last, but things are not working out. When the language school started in Kathmandu, we waited for our Nepalese visas while the oven, that is Delhi, turned its thermostat controls up notch by notch, for three months. We tried to learn Nepali from the textbook. We spent a month north of Delhi. We finally reached Nepal as the four-month course finished, tried to beat the language into our brains for two further months and then set off for Pokhara.

Brian has to take over as principal in a few weeks, but it is such a struggle to drag our small vocabulary into our minds to speak and listen to these friendly Nepali people. How will Brian know what is going on in the school? Limply in the monsoon humidity I unpack our belongings and sew curtains against the prying eyes at the bare windows.

The English teacher has tackled Brian in a staff meeting because he made the mistake of criticising some aspect of the Nepali education system. Other children tease Kaaren and Bronwyn on the 4-kilometre walk to the tiny expatriate school, and they and Adrienne have sores that refuse to heal in the damp heat. The water supply is erratic and the electricity has gone the same way. I am poor at shopping and cooking with the limited food and fuel available. My attempts at making bread are heavy work for the jaws and most meals unappetising. Brian and I think that is why his meals are distasteful and he feels discouraged every day, till we learn the tablets he is taking for mild amoebic dysentery cause a long-term bitter taste and depression.

Rosalind is a bright spot. Eleven months is a lovely age. She delights us with her gurgles and her beautiful blue eyes, as she crawls about our new stone house, only rarely falling down the stairs. She crows with joy from her high chair when, with six of us round the table, we sit down for meals.

Some nights we're glad when the current fails for the lights because we miss out on attracting the myriads of white moths that swarm through the unsealed gap between the ceiling and the wall. The sitting room is uninhabitable some evenings. We shut the door and sit in the bedroom and sweep up the moths in the morning. They are not ordinary moths, though. Their wings are so irritating that boys at the school who get one down their shirts itch for days. We try to avoid them.

But all these hassles pale beside what is happening to our laughing Rosalind.

Illness in the family

Kaaren watches one Sunday morning as I put Rosi down, whimpering fitfully, on the handloom bed cover.

'Mummy, why does her eye look like that?'

I take a second look. It's clouded right across, opaque over the bright blue iris and pupil.

'There's no sight in that eye,' I cry. 'What's happened? What's the matter with her eye?'

Quickly I grab her floppy pink bonnet against the glare outdoors, thrust Rosi into the blue pack and hoist her on to my back. Visit the school nurse. Short trip on the little motor bike to the Shining Hospital. Advised to go on to the government hospital. Wait with the Nepali mothers and their sick children on the verandah in the sticky noon heat. Ophthalmologist, injections, prescriptions, thorough examination under general anaesthetic, antibiotics, and then steroids every hour on the hour.

This is specifically a Pokhara disease. There are nine cases this September of mysterious and sudden loss of sight in one eye with acute iritis. Medical science can offer nothing. The treatments merely let us think something is being attempted. There seems to be some connection with the white moths, for the blindings happen only while they fly. An unrecorded virus or parasite perhaps?

And gradually the failure of the treatments sinks through to us. Brian realises it sooner than I do. We must sort this out with the One who gives us our orders.

The monsoon-swollen Seti River roars through its gorge below the Shining Hospital guest room. In the little blue cotton frock I had made, our sick baby girl lies on the low taped bed. We kneel on the flagstone floor.

'It feels like a dagger at the heart,' Brian says with tears in his eyes. 'Our littlest sweetheart.' The Seti River rumbles on.

'The treatment's doing no good. From a medical viewpoint she'll never see from her right eye again,' I murmur. But I keep hoping it is working. 'And we brought her to Pokhara. You could say it's our fault.'

We came here to help these disadvantaged people. For Brian to run a quality school for bright and disadvantaged boys. For us to encourage the tiny group of Christians. We are ready to tell the folk around about the God who loves.

Rosalind stirs and clasps my fingers as I gather her on to my lap. 'Are we willing for this kind of cost, Brian?'

'Do you remember the promise God gave me about the children as we left Ootacamund, dear?'

'I can't say I do.'

'It's one we've got to hang on to now. I believe it's for us, even though things are all going wrong. It's in Isaiah 40. "He tends his flock like a shepherd. He gathers the lambs in his arms and carries them close to his heart." God made the promise, and God will stand by it because we're asking him to look after Rosi.'

But another question hovers in my mind. Can we leave Pokhara after all? It doesn't look as if we're getting on very well. And now this dreadful health risk. Is it worth it? Shall we go on?

I try to pray with this in mind. No. It will not wear. Why the clear, very clear direction when we were still in Ootacamund? I cannot escape that. We can only accept. And so we pray for God to heal Rosalind's eye and ask that we will still be strong. Over and over we turn our minds to two things – the promise God gave us and the promise we gave that we would obey.

Our hearts ache even while our baby's health returns over the next four weeks, even as she smiles when we pick her up. Her eyes were so beautiful and now she smiles with only one. We need that assurance that the Great Shepherd looks after the lambs. God even sends an unexpected soothing to the raw edges of my spirit in the mouths of Nepali women who are complete strangers. When I carry Rosi on my back, they call out spontaneously, 'Kati ramro! Kati ramro!' (How beautiful!) They are words of healing to my hurt. God is watching over us. We can go on.

Misunderstanding

We can, and we do go on. But there is another dynamic that we do not talk about. It is too close to the heart of our own relationship for us to even analyse to ourselves while we are in the middle of it. It is the emotional understanding that may or may not come with the head understanding or even with the faith, and it came between us.

You see, Brian realised in the first few days that the sight in Rosi's right eye was gone and would never return. He experienced then the shock a parent feels at a child's permanent injury. I clutched at hope. I zealously administered treatments hourly day and night with the aid of an alarm clock: the drops to dilate the pupil and prevent the iris from adhering to the lens, the antibiotic, and the steroid.

Brian used to help by doing the 2.00a.m. to 5.00a.m. rounds. I half realised that there was little hope, but the reality had not got through to my emotions. I did not grieve. Brian, on the other hand, knew with both his head and his heart. He felt the hurt as Rosi totally lost the sight of her right eye. Kaaren told me later he cried with her about what was happening to Rosi. He could not understand why I seemed so heartless. I missed a chance to share the hurt with Brian. And Brian grew quiet and leaned harder on the promise that God, the Great Shepherd, would look after our little lamb.

When two weeks later the finality of what had happened got through to me, I cried for my baby. I looked for Brian's support and found he had already moved on. He had worked it out with God when I did not seem to feel. Then I had to take my own more lonely path. Find Jesus for myself. Ask God to help me cope. It was certainly less than ideal. At times in the past when Brian felt greatly upset I felt upset at the same time, but not this time. We may wish we could plan these things better, but somehow emotions do not come according to plan.

Something about a grief makes it a very private pain. Nobody else can feel it for you. I have spoken to another wife who, deeply distressed at her daughter's death, could not understand why her husband did not feel the hurt in the same way as her. He was a different person, and felt the hurt in a different way. She felt her path was lonely for years.

Perhaps it was good for me that I had to find Jesus in this for myself. When Brian died three years later I had to be strong on my own with Jesus. At least I had had a little practice.

One New Testament couple went through a physical disability that must have pushed at the limits of their faith and tested the strength of each to stand alone or together. And for them the timing of their learning was not always simultaneous. But they both came out stronger.

Zechariah and Elizabeth

A childless couple in the Western world today often feels a sense of failure and emptiness, and may feel that society looks down on them. That experience is multiplied several times over in a Muslim or Hindu society and was experienced just as deeply by people in Bible times such as Abraham and Sarah, Rachel before the birth of Joseph and Benjamin, and Hannah before the birth of Samuel. Elizabeth felt it so deeply she saw herself as in disgrace. Luke 1:25

Zechariah and Elizabeth were very good people. Luke 1:6 says they were righteous before God, living blamelessly according to all the commandments and regulations of the Lord. Probably Zechariah had only one chance in his lifetime to serve in the holiest place. He was from the right branch of the priestly tribe but even then was only selected in a draw among the priests.

The once-a-year ritual required him to sacrifice a bull for his own sins and then take a shovel of hot coals from the altar, sprinkle it with pungent incense till it smoked and take it through the curtain to the holy place so the cloud of incense covered the place of mercy. While he did this, the whole assembly of the people prayed outside the holy place.

Everyone's attention was fixed on pleasing God, but nobody expected a tangible visit, least of all Zechariah. When he saw an angel of the Lord, Gabriel, standing at the right of the altar of incense, he knew the meaning of terror. But Gabriel told him he would experience a different emotion – joy and gladness at the birth of a son whom he must call John. A son who, because he was filled with the Holy Spirit from his birth, would turn many people to the Lord their God, making ready a people for their God.

We cannot blame Zechariah for asking how this could be true when he was old himself and his wife was also getting on in years. But Gabriel's words proved true in a searing silence, just when he needed so much to tell what had happened. Dumb when people were so curious. And all he could do was wave his arms or write. How ambivalent he must have felt. Excited that the archangel Gabriel had appeared to him and promised a son, but ashamed that he was struck speechless at such a time for failing to believe the words.

But there was still a job to do. Zechariah would not be caught out a second time. It was his duty to continue to serve the full length of time at the temple, and he finished it out. He was already described as blameless in keeping the commandments and regulations. In the middle of all the questions that must have raced through his mind, Zechariah knew he must keep on with the given task.

Pregnancies and prophecies

Sure enough, new things were in store in their household. Four new things in fact, even before the angel's words came true. Elizabeth became pregnant and became a prophet. And their relation Mary visited and she too became a prophet. The turn of events must have come as a major shock in Jewish society. Elizabeth was filled with the Holy Spirit (Lk 1:41), the first person in the whole Bible specifically described as **filled** with the Holy Spirit, and a woman. Her prophecy was to affirm the task of another woman, and a young unmarried pregnant woman at that. Then the younger woman too gave a lengthy, powerful and even at times critical prophecy.

For now, though, people could have said madness had broken loose in the household of Zechariah and Elizabeth. Yet Elizabeth trusted the message that Zechariah said (or presumably wrote down) that he had heard. Zechariah must have trusted Elizabeth when she took a prophetic role that no one would have expected in a woman, and they both supported and sheltered lonely Mary in the enormous task she had accepted.

Spiritual sensitivity must have been one of Elizabeth's gifts. Otherwise, she would not have recognised her unborn son John's movement as a sign. God was using her as an instrument for revealing his plan. Perhaps she realised it. She must have been totally amazed.

> And Elizabeth was filled with the Holy Spirit and exclaimed with a loud cry, 'Blessed are you among women, and blessed is the fruit of your womb. And why has this happened to me, that the mother of my Lord comes to me? For as soon as I heard the sound of your greeting, the child in my womb leaped for joy. And blessed is she who believed that there would be a fulfilment of what was spoken to her by the Lord.

Elizabeth must have wondered why God gave her this gift of prophecy and not her husband, who would in the custom of the times, have been seen as the spiritual leader. It could have come between them. Zechariah was in trouble with God, publicly disgraced, and now she gets a miraculous gift when he is the one who is a priest.

Living with consideration

But no. Zechariah and Elizabeth seem to live with great consideration each for the other. She has been barren for years, but there never seemed to be a hint of annoyance from him. He spoke out of turn, and received a punishment from God, but she does not berate him. Perhaps with her older and pregnant, and him dumb, there were many ways in which they helped each over the next months. They do agree totally on how the child should be brought up as a Nazirite and on his name. They stand together in face of the pressure of their entire clan and acquaintances. They know each other so well that one can speak for the other.

Very likely other priests talk about their household while Zechariah and Elizabeth shelter an unmarried mother. Any explanations would be given by Elizabeth. When John is born, the neighbours and relatives wish to name the baby boy after his father, but Elizabeth takes a definite stand. 'No, he is to be called John.' Though they cannot accept her statement, Zechariah confirms it by writing the astounding, unfamiliar name.

That is really another development in their family dynamics. By force of circumstances when Zechariah cannot speak, Elizabeth becomes the spokesperson. Often where there is a physical disability or illness the dynamics of a family change. Different people shoulder responsibility. Even though Zechariah is normally the leader, he relies on Elizabeth for some of the lead when it is the obvious thing to do. Only when they have jointly insisted on the name given by God, is Zechariah's tongue freed. He praises God and brings the fear of God on their friends and relations by the obvious miracle taking place in front of them.

Then he experiences what Elizabeth has already felt – being filled with the Holy Spirit and prophesying. And already he knows the sort of life in store for John. Perhaps he has spent much time praying, or perhaps he is open there and then to receive the prophecy. God does not give prophecy to people who are not listening.

What a joining of minds and hearts for this devout couple – the only married couple in the Bible who were both filled with the Holy Spirit and both prophesied, with their prophecy recorded for future generations. What a conversation they would have that night after their friends and family left. And how their respect for each other and their desire to serve God must have grown.

There is something here for couples to look at as individuals, to learn lessons from God and to receive gifts for ministry to others. The timing is not always synchronised for both members of a couple to be at the same stage. Just in the same way as, when Rosi lost the sight in one eye, the timing when Brian and I grieved for the loss, and learnt from the Saviour, was not synchronised.

And Zechariah who first learned from God the plans in store for them, bungled the faith step, but still got the message through to Elizabeth so that they supported each other through the difficult months. Elizabeth grew and took more lead, she received the gift of the Holy Spirit and prophecy months ahead of her husband, but there was no envy, only a sense of wonder. One person moved ahead of the other in a spiritual gift, and exercised it for the good of others.

They rejoiced when their son came. Together they named their child. And God forgave Zechariah his mistake so thoroughly that he could now receive and give out an extended prophecy of joy and gratitude, faithfulness and foretelling.

It was a bumpy road for their marriage. Elizabeth and Zechariah had to walk alone at times. They each had to allow the other to grow stronger as an individual inside and outside the home, privately and publicly. But they both came through better able to serve each other, raise their child, minister the goodness of God to others, and praise their God.

We can learn from their example.

14

God's Call on the Life

Carolyn Kelly and Mark Johnston

'Kelsey was born one month premature, a difficult birth. She was a little cutie, but she upset all our expectations. She could scream for an hour at a time, day or night. It was so hard.'

The speaker is Carolyn Kelly and she and husband Mark Johnston are describing the adjustments as they worked out how they would cope with Christian ministry as well as their family life.

'Kelsey was very unsettled to begin with. She exhausted me. I was so tired I could hardly think. When I sat with other young mothers, I thought, "No wonder the conversations are limited to babies and knitting. We're all too tired."

'I went through a major personal crisis. I wanted to love the full-time mothering and worked hard at it. I loved being with Kelsey, but suddenly I was anonymous with few affirmations for my efforts. And I withdrew from the mental challenges I'd had before because I was so tired after the broken nights. I felt drained, and isolated by being at home. I told myself as I changed the sixth dirty nappy, "It's for my child. It has meaning." '

'I saw Carolyn going through this identity crisis,' Mark recalls. 'She'd moved from the stimulating world of student

Christian work to another world of mothering. She lost her identity as a worker, and asked "Who am I?" She longed to be in the student work, but found she could not do both roles.'

'We tried to continue sharing some of the job but it demanded travelling out of town, away for an evening or a weekend,' Carolyn continues. 'Only Mark could go. I had to re-evaluate who I was. A baby disrupted everything. I had this conflict in me that I wanted to keep doing the things I'd been doing, yet I simply wasn't able. I started to turn down offers of ministry or leadership.

'Two books helped me work through this – *Motherhood and God*, by Margaret Hebblethwaite, and *And Then there were Three*, by Sarah Wenger Shenck.'

'I felt Carolyn's struggle,' Mark adds in. 'We were in this together, so Carolyn's stress was my problem too. Yet I was still doing the work that she also loved to do.'

But the next crisis threw the couple into stress all over again, before they fully worked out the first one. When Kelsey was only nine months Carolyn found she was pregnant again. That threw her into a tailspin, she says. She was just getting her energy back and now she was to stay home with two babies. The early months of expecting Annelise were hard. She had to come to terms with her life.

'Yet when finally we came to the birth I was delighted,' Carolyn now enthuses. 'God was amazingly close to me in that experience as a woman. I kept thinking of the scriptures about God nurturing, taking special care of those with young. When, I was desperately thinking 'I'm not cut out for this caring for two babies,' I saw a vision of God carrying my children, tenderly watching over them. That really helped me through.'

As a father Mark again felt torn two ways. 'I had to do my work. Often I was counselling a student or attending a discussion and couldn't leave for home at 5.00p.m., and four times a year I had to go all week to conferences. I knew Carolyn hated being home on her own at those times. Sometimes I could arrange mornings working from home. I wasn't alone in these feelings. Friends felt the same stress when their profession made them work so hard and such long hours they could not fill their young family's need for time with them.'

At least Carolyn and Mark felt they were learning. They believed passionately that they did not need pre-set male or female roles. Now they were instead arranging their work more traditionally but seeing the tasks as equal and complementary. Still they found God prompted sometimes one with a decision to be made, sometimes the other – like the decision to continue in the student work a further year. Carolyn got the idea, even though Mark did the work. They had been running their partnership like that for years.

Drawn by common interests

Mark and Carolyn met at a conference when they were twenty-two. Carolyn, who had some years growing up in Singapore, had seen something of the world outside New Zealand, studied geography in Auckland and took an interest in justice and Third World development issues. Her family were very interested in education and ideas. She kept using her enquiring mind, never satisfied with pat answers, until it led her to choose to follow Christ during her first year at university. After that her constant question was, 'What's the impact of faith on my world? And on the world around me?'

When Mark, who grew up in a Presbyterian manse, finished his geography degree in Wellington, he left for a year working for the Church of North India in the Punjab, to explore his concern for mission and development issues. Not surprisingly the common interests helped draw them together when they met again while both did teacher training. They married the next year and took jobs teaching English, geography and social studies at a high school in the resort town of Rotorua. They worked there two years.

Job sharing

Then came a new job challenge – travelling work for the Tertiary Students' Christian Fellowship, helping students come to faith and grow in faith and bring the love of Christ to others. They shared hours and responsibility. Sometimes they divided the jobs geographically, often they travelled together. Sometimes they divided tasks on their strengths: Carolyn leading seminars, Mark doing administration. More often whoever was on the spot did the job as it occurred. Both counselled students.

Some people misunderstood the arrangement. Some assumed that Carolyn was only Mark's supportive helper, because of ideas of male leadership. The fact that Carolyn kept her family name, didn't draw many comments among the students, but it did with older folk.

'We didn't discuss it much at the start,' Mark comments. 'We just didn't see any need to change. But conservative Christian men ask me, "What's your wife doing with a separate name?" 'Isn't that a bit feminist?' Conversations seemed to imply, "Is this man okay theologically, if he doesn't keep his wife in order?" I felt their disapproval.'

Carolyn is more used to the feminist label. To her the word means a person who allows for the idea that men and women are equal in the sight of God. Some women acquaintances commented when she was expecting Kelsey, 'But you're so normal. I heard you were a feminist, but you're a nice person, and you're even pregnant!'

'If our names caused problems that truly hindered our ministry for God, we'd reconsider,' she and Mark continue. 'We want to fight the right battles on God's agenda, not ours.'

For the first few years of their marriage, equal sharing of decisions and equal responsibilities worked fine, first in teaching, and then as campus Christian workers. But that was before baby Kelsey was born. With her arrival, Carolyn laughs, all the tidy lifestyle went out the window.

'We thought we'd find a workable way to job-share around a baby,' says Carolyn. 'How wrong we were. I had something to learn about young babies. I was naive. Caring for Kelsey took so much time.'

Then it was Mark who felt prompted to change – they should plan towards full-time Christian work and apply for

Bible College. They lived with another family for six months to save money before they went. It was hard but worth it, they say.

Sharing the study options

Now, both studying, they have a challenge. Carolyn and Mark believe they felt God's call on their lives, on both their lives. Others observed they both had spiritual leadership gifts. But that does not mean plain sailing while they prepare for longer term Christian service. The most pervasive question they work on is parenthood. Caring for Kelsey, now 4 years, and Annelise, 2 years, has to be weighed up with pursuing the calling and gifting God gave. Each wants the support of the other's intellectual abilities. They enjoy theological exchanges at any time of the day or night in their rented apartment. Carolyn relishes the theology, wants to know why? And how? She is anxious to work out how Christian life is to be formed for herself and other women at the latter end of the twentieth century.

Mark wants to spend time enjoying his children – so small now, but they will grow so fast. Yet he is studying hard towards a degree in ministry. So is Carolyn. She ached inside when she first left the children for the lecture room, yet she believed she could not ignore the strong call to ministry that God gave her. Each feels the other has a destiny before God. They think of the contrast in the story Jesus told of the talents left wrapped and buried, or used out in the risky world. They believe they must not ignore their gifts.

Concluding they could not both study full-time, they decided Mark should do that one year and Carolyn the next, with the other studying part-time. Neither would complete their course in the two years, but they would both accomplish significant academic challenges while ensuring the children had a share of their time and energy.

They juggled lectures, child care and transport. They weighed up priorities every day, even their goals of equal opportunity. They are the more sure of their commitment to each other and the children. Carolyn now asked, 'What is our theology of family, and of parenthood?' She became convinced of the importance of family and of nurturing children in the early years.

'Motherhood matured me,' she says. 'I'd never been marginalised, pushed aside from where decisions are made, until then. It's given me a heart for other women and their struggles, the weight gain in pregnancy that they cannot lose, the loss of self-esteem, the difficulties of staying home all day.'

Family fun

If you have to stay with the children, you can decide to have fun, Mark and Carolyn concluded. Carolyn cooks with Kelsey, plays word games, stories, music, dancing to a music tape, going to the park. Mark colludes with the girls in make-believe with toys, makes kites to fly, reads stories or cooks dinner.

'I love it,' he grins. 'We play hide and seek, building a play hut, do the gardening or clean the car.'

His choice still draws comment. When Mark used to take the girls to the child health nurse for their check up, the nurse praised him, 'Isn't it wonderful how you men are starting to do this.'

'It's strange the reactions we get,' he muses. 'If men put me down with jokes implying I can't handle my stroppy wife, I think how Carolyn's not stroppy. We decided this together. Or people say I'm baby-sitting if I look after the children, as if they're not mine. Nobody describes Carolyn as baby-sitting. Some women tell Carolyn what a wonderful father and husband I am because I help with the children. That's nonsense. I'm just being a parent.

'I have lots of friends round my age, both Christian and secular, who want to, and do, play a sharing and caregiving role in parenting their children. And the variety of models of lifestyle for women is growing all the time. Despite our struggles, it would have been much harder doing this a generation ago. We're grateful for that.

'But our conservative Christian culture sometimes has great difficulty shedding gender stereotypes. Some men are uncomfortable if Carolyn gives a quick answer in class. If she makes a contrary point, even very politely, they may think she is aggressive. Yet the same question from a man could be asked abruptly and accepted easily.'

Talk of headship would make nonsense of Mark and Carolyn's situation, they say. They feel God uses the perceptions of both of them. Carolyn can say one day she respects Mark's study taking so much time, but she thinks it may be getting in between him and God. He thinks she is right. She suggests he take a half day retreat. Another time Mark may feel Carolyn is trying hard to get Kelsey's cooperation and pushing too hard. He suggests she hold back. It helps both mother and child.

'We keep talking about this all the time,' they muse. 'The challenge is to live new models where God may call women as well as men to do theology, to preach, to exercise authority. We keep working on how to live this out for our household, to follow Jesus on the road of obedience. If obedience is using the gifts God gave, our job is to keep finding out how to.'

And as we finish talking I ponder, Yes, that's what adulthood and parenting have to be like – working out answers together, each trying to do the best for one's part as a parent and in the world as a follower of Jesus.

My mind is moving on to the story of Mary and Joseph as they cared for each other and for baby Jesus. Joseph had the task of caring for Mary, and the highly significant task of acting as the human legal father of the Son of God and caring for him as his guardian. Mary's role, arguably the greatest parenting role in all of history, and one that changed the course of human history, was to bear baby Jesus and care for him. They were in it together, attempting to fulfill the call God had placed on their lives.

And when we study the story of the birth of Jesus from Luke 1–2 and from Matthew 1, significant points also show up in how decisions were made for that greatly honoured couple.

Mary and Joseph

He has lifted up the lowly

When the angel came to Mary, the first words were, 'Greetings, favoured one! The Lord is with you.' We wonder what may have gone before that would make the angel say this. Why was Mary favoured? Was her life already turned so much towards listening to and serving God that she was far more spiritual than the other young women? Was she wonderfully caring and considerate to her family and her neighbours?

The angel repeated similar words while she remained puzzled by the greeting, 'Do not be afraid, Mary, for you have found favour with God.' Does God have favourites, or had Mary earned any acclaim she received? In fact we know from her song in Chapter 1 that she certainly did not think she earned God's favour – 'He has looked with favour on the lowliness of his servant.' Lk 1:48

Mary supposed she received God's mercy because she feared him, 'His mercy is for those who fear him from generation to generation.' Lk 1:50

If we try to build a picture of Mary's circumstances when Gabriel visited her, we find little enough. Nazareth, where she lived, was an insignificant upland town between the Lake of Galilee and the Mediterranean Sea. From the slope above the town, where shepherd girls and boys could watch their flocks, Mary could look down however on a broad sweep of the history of her land. To the south lay the wide plain of Jezreel, scene of a number of battles of the Old Testament kings of Israel. To the south-west lay Mount Carmel, the reminder to any Jew of the God who met Elijah with fire and vanquished all lesser gods. On the east ran the Jordan river, first boundary of the land the Jews believed God had promised to them. Perhaps a sense of history entered into her soul and made her long for a saviour for her nation.

And perhaps Mary could read. She knew the scriptures so well that she could compose a song in the style of the Old Testament psalms, while putting in her personal feelings, joys and sorrows in a way so brilliant we're still singing it today. Her poetry was a prophetic gift from God, but maybe the words would come to her lips because she read enough to be soaked in the Old Testament. Illiterate women are not known for literary creativity on the scale of Mary's Magnificat.

The Jews prized a long written tradition giving very high status to their scriptures. Men could read. They learnt as boys at the Jewish schools run by the synagogues. Possibly fathers read the Old Testament to their families. We do know Mary's relation Zechariah could read and write. Mary is so steeped in the style of the Psalms that she must have read and sung them herself.

Reading trains the mind and would strengthen her personality. She was a thinker. Luke says later, 'She pondered these things in her heart.'

Surprisingly, we know nothing of Mary's parents. The genealogies in the New Testament, Matthew 1:5-15, Luke 2:4 and 3:23-31, show that Joseph was descended from King David, but tell us nothing about Mary's family. Her parents must have set up the usual arranged marriage for their daughter, and, although the young couple were engaged, the customs of their society probably would not let them talk together much, if at all.

Let it be with me according to your word

Here we come to a most amazing truth about Mary: the way she made decisions. The society of her time considered that a woman was in her father's care until she married and then in her husband's care. Western society (and most others) had the same view until very recent decades. Now here was a young woman, presumably still in her father's home, facing a momentous change of circumstances for herself, for her birth family and for the family she will join when she marries.

Unmarried and pregnant. That will bring much dishonour on both the families. Surely her father and her fiancé will need to be consulted. Surely nothing so enormous should happen without the consent of either or both of them. But the angel Gabriel goes directly to Mary, announces that she will conceive and bear a son, fills her in with some more detail and waits for her consent. And Mary, brave young soul and devoutly honouring to God, gives it with the words, 'Here am I, the servant of the Lord; let it be with me according to your word.' Lk 1:38

What really happens here? Is God, through Gabriel, really asking a woman, and a young one at that, to make a decision without asking her father or her husband-to-be? It looks like it. In fact by her independent response Mary shows she is more committed to obeying God than to obeying her father or her fiancé. She did not even ask her father or Joseph.

Even if an independent answer was not the custom, and is still not the custom in families dominated by fathers or husbands, her action is totally logical for a servant of God. Is this why God did not send Gabriel to Mary's father or to Joseph to ask permission for what God planned in sending his son into the world? What about the male head of the household? Should not someone make such an important decision for Mary? Apparently not.

God cut across all that people assumed about male headship by totalling ignoring it.

And this was big. After all, God was giving Mary the opportunity to be part of the decision on where the creator of the universe would appear in the world of human beings. The decision could hardly be greater. But it affected Mary more than anyone else, so God asked her to consent.

In fact Mary then made several more decisions, each without even apparently referring to her father or to Joseph. There is no indication elsewhere in the Bible that she was thought headstrong or insubordinate, either. Perhaps it was normal with her to decide for herself what she would do. And perhaps God showed approval of her actions by selecting her to be the mother of the Saviour with the message that she was highly favoured.

Acting independently

Here's what Mary did next. Without apparently discussing the journey with her father or Joseph, she hurriedly hiked off south to see Elizabeth and Zechariah. It is not clear which part of the hills of Judea they lived in, but the journey was 80 to 100 miles from Nazareth and would take perhaps three or four days. Then, she stayed about three months. Did she ask permission at home? We do not know. Perhaps the reported story omits some details, but the narrative records simply that a young woman made a decision to travel and carried it out.

And here's another puzzle. Did she travel all that distance alone? Probably not. Probably with the risk of highwaymen indicated by Jesus' later story of the good Samaritan, neither men nor women hiked the walking paths on their own. But even if she took with her a companion, brother, cousin, or father, the journey was taken at her initiative.

Mary later 'treasured all these things in her heart' for careful consideration. Perhaps she was very different from the other young women. Perhaps God chose her to be the mother of Jesus because she was a reader, a thinker, and independent in her actions.

And Joseph? Perhaps he was different too. When they were engaged, would it make any difference to him if Mary could read? He was willing to marry this unusual young woman without trying to assert his control over her. Maybe he appreciated her decision when she went off on such a long trek and stayed so long.

Matthew's gospel tells how Joseph did not at first fully understand or accept Mary's version of why she was pregnant. He needed his own visit from an angel. But he trusted her then, and trusted God. Joseph was willing to marry a woman who could probably read, who had things happening in her life that he could not understand, and who made decisions that he could not control.

And did he go further and recognise that God was calling Mary and him to a very special ministry that they would have to work on together? It looks like it. He totally followed the instruction of the angel and took Mary to care for as his wife, while asking no conjugal rights until she had borne the baby Jesus. He understood. He sheltered her from a bad name, gave her respect and care. And Mary joined forces with Joseph in the total commitment of marriage, apparently contented that they were in this God-called task together. They had learnt independently their tasks, and then together they would face the world supporting each other, and serving their Maker.

Serving God or human beings

Mary's task was more than to serve her husband's needs. She had to serve God. Joseph's task too was more than to make a living. He had to care for Mary and help to raise a very special son.

We do not know much more about Joseph's part during Mary's pregnancy. We do know he took her to Bethlehem, and was present during the delivery, and watching over her and baby Jesus when the shepherds came from the fields.

Joseph and Mary were so poor they offered only the poor folk's two turtle doves and two young pigeons when they took Jesus to be dedicated at the temple. They were both amazed when elderly Simeon prophesied that Jesus would be a light to the Gentiles and a glory to his people Israel.

But then Simeon did something most out of character for a Jewish man. He spoke in public to a woman, Mary, rather than to her husband. What can we draw from this? Perhaps Simeon too, with the knowledge revealed to him by the Holy Spirit who rested on him, knew that Mary was carrying out a task for God and, as such, drew his respect.

The latter part of the message, that a sword would pierce her own soul too, is the part one might expect to be given to a woman who would feel so deeply the emotional hurts of being the mother of a man misunderstood and put to death. But the first part of the message, the public part, that Jesus was destined for the falling and the rising of many in Israel, is what we might expect Simeon to tell the child's father. However Simeon told Mary. He did not relegate her in his thinking to the scenery that could not talk or think, though this happened to most women.

When Joseph took seriously the angel's order to escape from Herod by taking Mary and Jesus to Egypt, God commissioned him to protect Mary and Jesus. How they must have discussed their fears and hopes, these two, who together had the task of bringing up the Son of God.

And as we finish drawing fresh lessons from Mary and Joseph, we realise we have spotted three important facets worth weighing up. Mary was different. She was a young woman who thought hard, perhaps because she could read and make her own decisions as well as living humbly in her spirit. Joseph and Mary each had a task from God. And, perhaps most remarkable of all, God sent the angel Gabriel to a lone young woman to consent in a decision as momentous as where the Saviour of the world would be born.

15

Small is Beautiful

Shared intimacy

While we have considered all through these chapters how couples make decisions, we must also look at the intimacy that draws them together to start with, and acts as the glue that keeps them together. Then we'll look at two vastly different sections in first the Old Testament and then the New Testament showing aspects of intimacy.

Intimacy didn't appear readily as I interviewed couples. Perhaps that is not surprising. Part of intimacy is something couples keep for each other alone, but another part goes unnoticed – the myriad shared experiences, the little things that would mean nothing to anybody else anyway. They are the things two people enjoy together, or even suffer or work for together. Perhaps just the two of them, sometimes with their children, sometimes with extended family or friends.

Let me describe some of the visible intimacies and shared moments on which Brian and I built our togetherness. They'll serve as examples of moments of understanding that form the matrix and warmth of living together.

The alarm goes off at 6.00a.m. in our village house in Nepal. The room is starkly basic to Western eyes, though to village eyes generously furnished – plank bed frame, plank floor, stone walls, more planks for the door, cotton bedding, a cupboard. Brian pads down the half-light stairs to tinker with the temperamental kerosene (paraffin) primus, put on a pan of water and eventually negotiate the stairs again with a cup of tea for me to sip over my morning Bible reading. Our own little ritual, his chance to show he cares.

I am driving the little green Honda on the clay track. How is the petrol? Not too low yet, but I take the time to go over to the shed and get it filled for Brian. He uses the motorcycle more than I, but he is always in such a rush to get to the Education Office in town, or see some official on school business. And there is no phone.

We are scurrying back to the house after the 8.00a.m. village church service on Saturday and due to meet friends in town to go walking up Sarankot Ridge with the children. But church ran late, the breakfast dishes are still on the table and we must get the picnic and the children ready. Brian's natural inclination, if the electricity is on, is to go to the little turntable and put on some Bach organ music while we get ready. It soothes his mind. But I cannot handle Bach organ music when I am in a rush. It makes me feel stressed and upset.

I think of it days later. Brian must have ignored his urge for Bach because he remembered it did not help me. I got through the rushed three-quarters of an hour without grumbling at anyone.

Intimacy can be one person putting himself or herself out to help the other. Like the time in New Zealand when Brian wanted cricket flannels and hoped I would make them because that would be so much cheaper than buying them. I wonder now why I agreed to make them. They were so much work – buy the pattern, buy the cream fabric, and learn how to make men's trousers when I'd never sewn them before. I managed to produce some good trousers at quarter the shop price, but then I learnt that bowlers rub the bright red ball on the cream trousers to smooth one side and increase the spin! And who was going to wash the red off them?

Or what about the time I went to buy fruit trees for our back yard in Auckland and was taken in by the nurseryman's sales pitch. 'Sure, you can grow guavas in Auckland. These are great guava trees.' I knew guavas, the big six-centimetre tropical kind, were Brian's favourite fruit. I bought two trees and planted them triumphantly in our garden – especially for Brian. How mistaken I was. The fruit were tart little one-centimetre berries. They're growing there still – a failed but genuine attempt to do something to make Brian happy.

Part of our intimacy was increasingly sharing our family and relations, occasions especially relished because time with them was so sparse between our years away from New Zealand. Brian shared my relations by challenging my brother-in-law to tennis the morning before he married my sister, or spending long hours discussing the conundrums of the book of Hebrews with my father, or washing the dishes after a family dinner, or loading hay with my brother or making music with my sister.

When Brian's sister needed to learn to drive, I took her out in our blue car to practise on the road, and when Brian worried about his mother's health, we discussed her needs together.

We liked to have someone to sound out our ideas on. I tried to analyse with Brian in what sense ambition was a Christian virtue, or Brian would try out his ideas on why Christians can still sin, and how they feel about it. We had both, after all, worked on divinity degrees. And then when Brian was principal in Pokhara he talked over with me how he could handle the competing needs of the various departments in the school: the hostels, the academic life, the school farm, the accounts, the building department.

Of course a couple in mission work together, is in it as a couple – both need to keep their own devotional life alive and to help others. We read and prayed on our own in the mornings, and read a few verses of the Bible and prayed together in the evenings. These were times when we talked over what we thought, prayed about needs, or often, tired after the day, just prayed for each other, the children and our families at home.

For Christian work I volunteered to write the cross-references for the Nepali Bible. Many an evening when the power went off, I sat up in bed with two candles on the plaster window ledge behind and searched through my books. Brian accepted my devotion to the task. He sat up on the other side of the bed and typed letters – until we could not stand the work any longer and snuggled up under the covers.

On Friday nights, with the help of a keen young convert who ran around the village calling his Hindu friends to come to our house, we ran a Bible study. Reading Nepali script by candle-light was Brian's pet hate, but he would wrestle through the preparation while I wrestled with the primus to stew up some sweet dust tea for the boys. We were supporting each other towards the same goals.

It is a great strength to any marriage if a couple have the same ideas about leisure. We both preferred a hike and a picnic far ahead of going out to dine, even though dining was cheap in the little Nepali restaurants. Walks were some of our most precious family times, our family together, or with friends, away from the calls of people and work. Sometimes we went out for days at a time. Pleasures become very simple then – just the cessation of the pull of the pack on the shoulder muscles and a rest for tired feet. Quote of the week from Brian: Pleasure on a trek is a drink of water, a rest, shade, girls to laugh with and a wife to smile with.

And we loved to enjoy friends together. Friends who sat up late talking. In the winter in our village we felt it was a Christian virtue, in order to save forests, not to burn firewood unnecessarily. So although it was cold we merely offered our guests a blanket each if we sat round chatting on a chilly night.

Sometimes we had to accept each other's idiosyncracies. Brian tried so hard to learn Nepali fast that he spoke even if he got it wrong. I squirmed when I noticed the mistakes, but I said little, as I was trying to get it right. I did not learn to speak nearly so soon. Our styles were different. Either of us could criticise. But it was more important to allow for differences.

At times there was work to make up for someone's mistake, like the time I hurriedly baked biscuits before we went out on a Saturday, and remembered when we had walked one hour up the river that I had left the little electric oven turned on. Brian ran back and turned it off and pulled out the black cinders that remained. He did not grumble at me about it.

But we needed to give each other room to be different too. Brian used to read to the girls comic strip books about the intrepid explorer, Tintin, or the pseudo-Latin character, Asterix. They dramatised and laughed and I could not get interested in the stories at all. I could not understand the attraction and initially felt irritated. It was better if I just went and did something else and let Brian and the children enjoy that bit of fun.

We laughed together about lots of other things. The village boy who decided to have a repeat of stomach-ache because I once gave him fizzy fruit salts. The time a shrew fell in a jug and swam around with little beady eyes above the milk, and the time a snake slid into the kitchen and about 22 villagers crowded in with sticks and could not find it behind the cupboards, so we ate our dinner sitting cross-legged on our chairs.

Another time somebody accidentally kicked the chamber pot the girls kept in the upstairs loft bedroom. It spilt and leaked through into the bedroom where guests were staying. Shamefaced giggles! That loft was a trap in more ways than one. The roof was not high enough for us adults, and I continually thumped my head so hard on the rafters that I sat half stunned on the floor while Brian rushed upstairs and sympathised. Then we laughed as he sat on Rosalind's tiny bed for bedtime stories and hugs, and the bed cracked under his weight.

And of course feeling proud of your children is a wonderful aid to intimacy. One magical moment arrived in the middle of a thunderstorm. Pokhara has spectacular storms. Tempests. The dry, dusty ground becomes a distant memory with the first week of rain in June. Lightning and thunder crash, and rain turns the village green temporarily into a shallow lake.

That was the signal for our girls to put on their swimsuits and race out into the deluge, skidding in the wet grass, jumping into the overflowing watercourses, laughing and shouting in the haze as day softened into evening. One late afternoon three fair-haired little girls dashed outside sliding in the puddles, skating along the grass. Brian and I stood watching from the verandah with our hearts hovering towards our children as dusk and mist and joy of youth blended.

We stood spellbound as Bronwyn, Adee and Rosi joined hands and ran skipping and dancing till they grew fainter across the fading green. Our eyes met. We wanted the children to face life like that – with energy and vitality and the security of a loving home and a heavenly Father.

And now when I look back over the things that held Brian and me together, and I am sure the same things hold many others, the shared times gain their own beauty, and I remember again that small is beautiful.

I have since read that there are six kinds of intimacy: emotional, social, sexual, intellectual, recreational, and spiritual. Most of our shared times fit into one or other of those important categories.

But along with them all one of the most powerful ingredients is loyalty. You stick by each other and you plan to make your life together work, whether the emotion ebbs or flows. The strongest and simplest compliment a wife or husband pays to a marriage comes, with arms about the other, saying, 'This place, with you, is where I really belong.'

•

An Old Testament intimacy

One extended passage of the Bible, the Song of Solomon, shows the intimacy of a man and a woman in love at sufficient length to portray how they initiate actions and romance. They do so equally. 'Let him kiss with the kisses of his mouth,' it starts off. 'Draw me . . . We will exult and rejoice in you,' the girl exclaims to the lover.

'Your cheeks are comely with ornaments, your neck with strings of jewels,' he praises her good looks and her aids to beauty.

She leads him on unashamedly. 'While the king was on his couch, my nard gave forth its fragrance. My beloved is to me a bag of myrrh that lies between my breasts.'

She coos, 'I am a rose of Sharon, a lily of the valleys.'

He brags, 'As a lily among the brambles, so is my love among maidens.'

She searches for him in the streets of the town until the watchmen laugh at her. 'Scarcely had I passed them, when I found him whom my soul loves. I held him and would not let him go.'

He is so full of sentimental thoughts he runs through a spiel of poetic metaphors. 'How sweet is your love, my sister, my bride! How much better is your love than wine, and the fragrance of your oils than any spice! Your lips distil nectar, my bride; honey and milk are under your tongue.'

Further on she instigates a lover's walk in the country, leading to a consummation. 'I am my beloved's and his desire is for me. Come, my beloved, let us go forth into the fields, and lodge in the villages; let us go out early to the vineyards, and see whether the vines have budded, whether the grape blossoms have opened and the pomegranates are in bloom. There I will give you my love.'

No false modesty for this young woman. She knows she can give pleasure and she knows she can receive it. They are partners, delighting in every minute together, leading each other on, one and then the other. He is infatuated up to the eyeballs, and so is she. No playing hard to get. No playing passive. They are each actively drawing delight from their love-making.

And if we stop to draw the conclusions from their enchanted world of each other, we find neither is dominant, neither always takes the lead. That would decrease their fun by half, if one always initiated and the other always complied. In these, the fondest love scenes in the whole Bible, the lovers are patently mutually active.

Intimate decisions in the New Testament

The Bible chapter to examine now is 1 Corinthians 7, a chapter largely ignored in discussion about the relation between men and women in marriage. It applies primarily to couples making decisions about their sex life, but it holds for us an extraordinary underlying symmetry. At each point where a couple decides on an action, and this at the deepest, most intimate points of their marriage, one statement gives half of the decision to the man and another statement, spelt out, gives the other half of the decision to the woman. Let us look through these amazingly symmetrical verses.

Apart from a few asides, I shall let the Bible speak for itself. Whenever Paul considers a behaviour for one party in a marriage, he considers the equivalent behaviour, as a separate personal option, for the other.

Verses from 1 Corinthians 7

Because of cases of sexual immorality, each man should have his own wife and each woman her own husband.

'The husband should give to his wife her conjugal rights, and likewise the wife to her husband.' These sexual decisions, at the very core of a marriage, where it's finally 'at' in the relationship, are made with total equality.

'For the wife does not have authority over her own body, but the husband does; likewise the husband does not have authority over his own body, but the wife does.' Do the proponents of male leadership as the rule for Christian families know that verse is in the Bible? Equal authority over each other's bodies.

'Do not deprive one another except perhaps by agreement for a set time, to devote yourselves to prayer, and then come together again.' The mutual agreement again.

'The wife should not separate from her husband (but if she does separate, let her remain unmarried or else be reconciled to her husband), and the husband should not divorce his wife. If any believer has a wife who is an unbeliever, and she consents to live with him, he should not divorce her. And if any woman has a husband who is an unbeliever, and he consents to live with her, she should not divorce him.' This requires respect, one for the other as a person who is one's equal.

'The unbelieving husband is made holy through his wife, and the unbelieving wife is made holy through her husband.

'Wife, for all you know, you might save your husband. Husband, for all you know, you might save your wife.

'Let each of you lead the life that the Lord has assigned, to which God called you.

'The unmarried man is anxious about the affairs of the Lord, how to please the Lord; but the married man is anxious about the affairs of the world, how to please his wife, and his interests are divided. And the unmarried woman and the virgin are anxious about the affairs of the Lord, so that they may be holy in body and spirit; but the married woman is anxious about the affairs of the world, how to please her husband.'

Yes, the Bible says a wife's role is to please her husband. And in the same paragraph we find the husband's role is to please his wife. When I read all those verses one after another I feel hit by a series of hammers. Equal, Equal. Equal, Equal.

The very fact that the author goes to great lengths to keep each statement equally accountable for women and men is remarkable, and an indication to readers that this is important. But the contents of the instructions are also noteworthy and unexpectedly different from the common view that Paul expected husbands to make the rules while wives just went along. The writer is talking about the most important decisions: whether to marry, whether to remain married, how to make decisions on sexual behaviour within marriage, who controls whose body, how far a couple will together allow their spiritual life to impinge on their marriage. What more central issues could arise?

The whole chapter is a thrilling discovery. Hundreds of Christian couples with healthy marriages have already put it into practice. Finding it is actually in the Bible allows them to bring their theory of how a biblical marriage works into line with their practice. They no longer need to pretend that the man as the ultimate authority is God's order in marriage. And for husbands and wives who practise an unequal partnership in which either or both members are less than adult and not taking full responsibility for their decisions before God, a challenge now arises. Can we re-shape our partnership for mutual submission, mutual decision making and mutual encouragement to grow?

The model in the Bible is: The wife does not have authority, but the husband does; the husband does not have authority, but the wife does.

STUDY GUIDE

A Casebook Of Bible Marriages

Exploration of the lives of husbands and wives found in the Bible

BEULAH WOOD

Ten studies for groups
or couples on the
decision-making of
Bible husbands and wives

A Note to the Reader

The information in these studies could have been written as Bible teaching but I have chosen to write it as studies for several reasons.

- The Bible is our foundation for both faith and action. If we want to learn how God wants us to act, we must start there and apply it to our day.
- If I give as teaching the conclusions I reach, readers could rightly say, 'That's just what she thinks.' But when you as a reader discover the impact of a Bible passage for yourself, you will be ready to accept it.
- When you discuss a Bible study you cannot skim through it. You have to slow down and think, and that helps in remembering it later.
- When you study the Bible with somebody else, discussing together what you are learning, you can then help each other to put into practice the things you learn.
- And do pray at the finish. The Lord God is the one who can help us act on what we learn.

A Note to the Study Leader

These studies are appropriate for couples to use together as they work to understand and put into practice a biblical view of marriage.

They are also applicable for group study when a good number is eight or ten people. This is a number that can build a group identity meeting regularly, probably once a week. People can begin to support one another, learn from each other and take ideas from one another. The group interaction itself is important because how the people respond to the truth they are learning influences others who are on the same journey.

Each session will take about one and a half hours, and it is not necessary to use only the questions given. They may spark useful illustrations or comparisons from among the group, and these should be encouraged. It is not essential to cover all questions if some are not relevant to the group, but the commitment to action should be included so that people plan actions as a result of their learning.

A study could spread over more than one session if the participants want to discuss more.

If several members are able, they could take a turn to lead the study, but the leader must clearly understand the study beforehand and be able to keep the discussion on track. Encourage all members to contribute and treat all contributions with respect.

Table of Contents

Prologue

When I decided to study the marriages of the Bible, I made some remarkable discoveries. I found the reality of the way God dealt with husbands and wives was far from the stereotype I had accepted as an evangelical Christian that the husband always leads and the wife submits.

I didn't know the study would be such fun.

I laughed when I found that God chose Deborah not only for a day to inspire an army, but as national leader for 40 years, although she was a married woman and one who in her day would expect to be under her husband's authority. Abigail flagrantly went against her husband's wishes and was praised for her efforts, while he was struck dead. And a king sent five privy councillors to the prophet Huldah for advice, without so much as a 'by your leave' to her husband Shallum.

My daughter Adrienne, when she was seventeen, spotted the amusing story about the parents of Samson, Manoah and his wife. That man really wanted to know what was going on, and the angel of the Lord kept talking to his wife and not to him.

When I studied the Bible, I found stories in which husbands and wives shared the tasks of life, stories which showed God relating to women as if they were required to think, decide, carry out responsibilities with or without the permission and assistance of husbands, and also stories illustrating the problems of some married couples who did not decide together.

Here is the argument. There's still much teaching from pulpits, Christian radio, books, that a woman should obey her husband, or that he should make the decisions for the family.

If a woman must obey her husband, she could stand before Christ and, when asked why she did not teach a Sunday School class, reply, 'My husband didn't want me to, so I obeyed him. Isn't that what you wanted, God?' She would then step behind her husband and let him answer for her.

But this is not what we believe. We believe all human beings must receive the rewards or punishments of their own actions. We believe God holds each of us accountable for our actions and we will all stand before the judgment seat of Christ. Romans 14:10

This set of studies explores the ways God expects both men and women to be accountable for their actions.

Study One

Adam and Eve

Aim: to examine God's plan for Adam and Eve, and what happened when they broke God's law.

A Exploring your experience

1. Do you think husbands and wives these days influence each other noticeably to do good or to do wrong?

B Life and Times

This is an important study. The way God made Adam and Eve to relate to each other and to him sets the tone for future people in their responsibilities to him and to each other.

Adam and Eve have been used to back very diverse theories of marriage relationship, so we need to let the text speak to us. How God treated them as accountable for their actions is also an important study.

C Biblical Reflection
Genesis 1:27-28, 2:18, 23-25, 3:1-21

2. What was unique about God's creation of the first human male and female as compared with the rest of creation? What does this say about the value of woman and man?

3. When God made humans, both male and female were made in God's image. This indicates that the sense in which man and woman were like God was not in their physical attributes. What does this say about whether men or women can claim to be more like God than the other?

4. Why did God create the woman? What does this say about the relationship between men and women?

Note: The word translated 'helper' in 2:18 could be more correctly translated assistant, advisor or consultant. In this sense it is used in the Bible 15 times to describe God the Father or the Holy Spirit bringing relief and aid in a time of need. Does this speak for today about the relationship of husband and wife?

5. What meaning do you take from 'one flesh' in 2:24?

6. Did Adam and Eve each have free choice about whether they obeyed or disobeyed God?

7. When God returned, the couple blamed each other. What had changed in their relationship?

8. In the list of punishments, often called the 'curse', which things affected the relationship of the man and woman?

D Analysis

9. What can you infer about their relationship to each other and their surroundings when Adam and Eve were not ashamed of nakedness 2:25? And when they needed to wear clothes 3:7,21? How had the loss of innocence affected them?

10. Some say Eve sinned because she handled a situation without asking her husband's advice. Discuss this view with reference to single women and solo mothers.

11. In 2:18,24,25 Adam and Eve were partners in pleasure. From 3:7-8 they were partners in guilt. Did God treat them as equally responsible for their actions in the sense that they were both punished? If the husband was totally responsible for the

couple's decision, would not God have punished only Adam? Does it seem fair if the husband and wife each receive praise or blame for their actions in God's sight?

12. The New Testament claims that Jesus takes away the effect of the 'curse' Galatians 3:10-13 – thorns in farming, and pain in childbirth remain. Women being ruled by husbands was part of the 'curse'. Gen 3:16 Was it lifted in the New Testament? What things DID Jesus change?

E Commitment to action

13. If God sees husbands and wives as equally responsible for their actions, how can a couple treat themselves and each other as equally responsible?

14. If men and women are equally responsible for their actions, do you think a woman's marriage vows should be the same or different from a man's?

F Couple's questions

15. Do we each see the other as made in the image of God? In what ways?

16. Do we ever 'blame' the other for actions we were really responsible for ourselves?

17. Does one member ever try to hide behind the other, avoiding responsibility?

G Prayer

We praise you, Saviour, that we no longer live under the 'curse'. May we each practise wisely our freedom and responsibility.

H Link work this week

Write a set of marriage vows that gives partners equal responsibility.

Study Two

Abraham and Sarah

Aim: to examine the failed relationships both in the system of the patriarchs, and in patriarchy reversed, and to identify a better approach.

A Exploring your experience

1. Thinking about work, holidays, home, clubs, have you ever experienced a situation where one person made a wrong decision affecting other people, when if only others had been consulted it could have been avoided?

B Life and Times

The patriarchal system, which applied to Hebrews, Greeks and Romans, placed control in the hands of men and treated women as little more than children who had all major decisions made for them. This culture has influenced Christianity and also appears strongly in modern days in other religions and cultures.

God had promised Abraham in Genesis 12:2, 13:16, 15:1-6 that he would establish a nation. He and Sarah had waited decades. They needed a son. Besides this, ancient culture placed a heavy burden on women and men. They were failures in life if they had no child. (This was more often blamed on the woman.)

Section 1: Abraham leads

C Biblical Reflection
Genesis 12:10-20, 20:1-18

1. How was the decision reached that Sarah would be known as Abraham's sister? Genesis 12:10-20

2. This occurred a second time. Genesis 20:1-18 What had they failed to learn?

3. What were the results of the one-person decision in the marriage? Who gained and who lost in the strategy?

D Analysis

4. Romans 14:10 says we must all stand before the judgment seat of Christ. This means Christ will treat every person as responsible for their own actions. Can Abraham alone be considered responsible for the action, or both of them? Should Sarah have objected and told the truth?

5. How could the decision have been differently made?

6. What are the disadvantages of one person dominating in a marriage, or of one adult taking responsibility for the decisions of another adult? Could you say that person is treated as a child?

E Commitment to action

9. What can we do to help dominant marriage partners to understand the disadvantages of taking away another's right to decisions?

10. In what ways can we help women or men whose partners make all the major decisions, whether appropriate or inappropriate?

F Prayer

Pray for men and women to build strong marriages with shared decision making.

Section 2: Sarah leads

C Biblical Reflection
Genesis 16:1-6,15; 21:1-14

In section 1, we saw Abraham decide without Sarah. Now Sarah pushes Abraham into a decision.

1. Sarah, in desperation, took the decision that she would have a surrogate child through her slave girl, Hagar. What do you think of the way in which the decision was made? Abraham seems to have accepted Sarah's decision against his better judgment. Was this faith?

2. God had already praised Abraham for his faith, 15:6. Who was lacking in faith now, one or both?

3. In 16:5-6 Sarah blamed Abraham for the fact Hagar was proud to be pregnant. How did he attempt to shrug off responsibility?

D Analysis

4. Did either care to treat Hagar as a person rather than a thing?

5. In 21:10,11 did either Sarah or Abraham accept the implications of the past action?

6. Sarah by her jealousy for her son to inherit Abraham's wealth forced Abraham to nearly cause the death of both Hagar and Ishmael, though God overruled. Again, which of them treated Hagar as a person?

7. When analysed, the situations of Genesis 12:10-20, 20:1-18 and 16:1-6 show Abraham making decisions without discussion with Sarah, and then Sarah making plans without bothering about Abraham's faith that God would answer their need for a

son. Do you agree that the conclusion to draw is that without discussion their decisions brought disaster?

8. How could Abraham and Sarah have improved their communication with each other and their joint decision making? Where might they have brought God into the decision?

E Commitment to action

9. How can we in our marriages make joint decisions and jointly accept responsibility for them? How can we avoid passing the buck when something turns out wrong?

10. How can we avoid treating people as things?

F Questions for couples

11. We're not as bad as Abraham and Sarah, but did we make some of their mistakes? (Confessions here, not accusations!)

12. How can we improve?

G Link work this week

Deliberately cooperate with someone else in a joint decision.

H Prayer

God of Abraham and Sarah, help us as couples to trust you like Abraham, to seek for answers like Sarah, but not to push the decisions of one on the other.

Section 3: Optional Extension work on two difficult passages

Genesis 21:8–20

Sarah, wanting to send Hagar off into the desert, was heartless. But God did two surprising things. He let it happen; and he told Abraham to do whatever Sarah suggested.

1. Why did Sarah want to remove Ishmael?

2. In view of God's long-term plan, why did Ishmael have to go? How did God comfort Hagar and Ishmael?

3. God could have told Abraham to send Ishmael away. Instead, the initiative came from Sarah. We can only guess, but what might have been the reasons why God told Abraham to obey Sarah?

4. In any case, it surprises us that God on this occasion told the great patriarch to obey his wife. What might we learn from this?

1 Peter 3:5–6

5. Peter says that Sarah obeyed Abraham, and then tells Christian women to obey their husbands in the same way. This is shocking if we remember that Abraham told lies about Sarah to save his own skin, and consequently twice caused her to be put at risk in the harem of a heathen king. Should a woman obey such a husband?

6. Our study showed that, on at least one occasion, God told Abraham to obey Sarah. Perhaps the instruction to obey their husband, as Sarah did, was not such a blanket rule after all! What do you think?

7. Some people say that if there is more than one person in control of a family, it causes confusion. Joint decisions do take longer to work through. Can anyone in the group give an example of joint decision-making by a group of people sharing accomodation, or involved in team ministry, for example? How are decisions achieved?

8. None can doubt that one-person decisions have caused untold pain and destruction in marriages in every country of the world. Think of the ravages of alcoholism, wife-beating, adultery, waste of income, drugs, selfishness, greed and divorce, when one partner refuses to consider the other. How might we answer those who say husbands must be in control?

Study Three

Isaac and Rebekah

Aim: to examine the problems in another patriarchal family, discovering a cause of deceit and manipulation.

A *Exploring your experience*

1. Have you ever felt that someone near to you needed to make a decision in a certain direction, but been convinced they would do the opposite? What did you do?

B *Life and Times*

When the Hebrews were hardly yet a separate tribe among the many desert tribes, and when the survival of everybody in the desert depended solely on supplies of water for the herds and crops, Isaac's workers often competed with the workers of local chieftains for access to water. Genesis 26:15-22 Relationships were sensitive. Isaac did not want fights between the workers, nor to have to mount a military defence of his wife from other chiefs.

Isaac and Rebekah were relatives. She was the daughter of Isaac's first cousin Bethuel, the marriage having been arranged, at the request of Isaac's aging father, Abraham, by his reliable old household manager. Isaac fell in love with Rebekah after they were married. We do know that Rebekah was willing for the marriage.

C Biblical Reflection
Genesis 26:6-11, 27:1-16, 41-28:1

2. In what way did Isaac and Rebekah follow Isaac's parents? Who gained? Who lost? Which people who did not worship Jehovah knew better than they did?

3. What does chapter 27:1-16 tell us about Isaac and Rebekah's relationship? Did they trust each other? Do you think they talked much?

4. How honestly had Isaac and Rebekah discussed the future and the well-being of their sons? What can happen when parents have favourites?

D Analysis

5. Why did Isaac deceive Rebekah? Why did Rebekah deceive Isaac? Why did she become manipulative? Could she influence the family decision in a fair way?

6. Do you know of women who deceive or manipulate in your own society? Are their reasons similar to Rebekah's? What is the result?

7. Isaac and Rebekah's family was in a mess. How could this have been prevented or changed?

E Commitment to action

8. How could we educate and help couples to avoid one person dominating and the other becoming manipulative?

9. How can we encourage husbands and wives to communicate more and to share decision making?

F *Questions for couples*

10. Has either of us favoured one child more than another?

11. Has either of us had a fixed plan of action and refused to listen to the other's reasoning?

12. Have we ever resorted to manipulating the other? Perhaps even unconsciously? Can we forgive each other now, and determine to avoid trying to get our own way by deceit?

13. What can we do to improve our communication so that our relationship is not harmed by either failing to talk or failing to listen?

14. How can we best plan our assistance to our children as they grow older?

G *Prayer*

Pray for women or men who have lost control of the decisions that affect their lives. Pray for more honest talking and understanding in our homes and for shared decisions.

H *Link work this week*

15. Choose a time to LISTEN to your partner on a topic that affects the family.

Study Four

Deborah and Lappidoth

Aim: to understand the task and the family life of Deborah who was married to Lappidoth and called to become a national leader.

A Exploring your experience

1. Have you ever said, 'Why doesn't somebody DO something?' about your community, your church, your city? This must have been how Deborah felt. Have you ever tried to persuade somebody else to do something when they thought they could not? Have you ever done it yourself because you knew it needed doing?

B Life and Times

At this stage the nation of Israel had no king but was ruled by judges who also organised the people to fight against the enemies who surrounded them and kept up a pressure on control of the land.

Othniel had ruled for 40 years, then Ehud was the national champion against the people of Moab. Other champions were Gideon and Samson in a cycle of deliverance followed by peace, followed by the people turning away from God and incurring

God's punishment at the hands of warriors in battle till he had mercy on them again and raised up another deliverer.

We have no background on how Deborah came to be known as a prophet, nor why she was known as a judge. Although she was the only woman up to this date recorded as carrying these roles, her position does not seem to be questioned. In this study, we will attempt to detect her relationship to Lappidoth while she carried out these tasks.

C Biblical Reflection
Judges 4:1-16, 5:1-5,11-13

2. In the story, what were the functions of:
   (a) Sisera, (b) Deborah, (c) Lappidoth, and (d) Barak?

3. What knowledge and action by Deborah shows her to be a prophet of the Lord?

4. What might Lappidoth and Deborah have discussed previously that would:
   (a) Make it possible for Deborah to work so closely with Barak, even going off to war with him, without apparent reference to Lappidoth?
   (b) Enable Lappidoth to trust Deborah to take a position as a military and national leader?
   (c) Enable Lappidoth to trust Deborah without envying her position or requiring a decision-making position in the family?

5. What was Deborah's major initiative, and why did she do it?

6. Would Deborah or Barak alone have been successful? What does this say about teamwork?

D Analysis

7. Some people say God uses women as leaders only if the men fail to lead. If this were so, what would Deborah's action in sending for Barak and giving him orders say about Lappidoth, Barak, the men of Israel?

8. Would a woman like Deborah who was in touch with God dare to lead if doing so implied a criticism of all the men of God in her community?

9. So why did God call a woman to lead?

10. Apparently the fact that Deborah had a husband and there were already male leaders in Israel was irrelevant. If God calls a woman to lead in church or civil administration today, what are:
 (a) the advantages, (b) the disadvantages?

11. If God calls a man to lead, what are:
 (a) the advantages, (b) the disadvantages?

12. The task in fact needed action by both Deborah and Barak, as well as the people who went out to fight. What can we learn from the joint leaders (Deborah and Barak) in their recognition of:
 (a) the work of the people? 5:1-2
 (b) the work of God? 5:11-13

13. Deborah became one of the judges who ruled Israel. She ruled for 40 years. What indication do we have in 5:31 that this woman judge did the country much good?

In fact, since she ruled 40 years, she must have been young at the start. A young married woman probably meant having young children too. She and Lappidoth must have made some arrangement for the smooth running of the household and family in order for her to apportion her time to sit under the palm tree and give decisions in national disputes. They must have learnt much about joint decision making.

E Commitment to action

14. How can we improve our teamwork of men and women:
 (a) in relationships at home?
 (b) in our communities?
 (c) in our churches?

F Questions for couples

15. If this was our marriage what would we have wished we had talked over beforehand?

16. What would we want to talk over when it was all finished?

17. How can we improve our communication so that we will trust each other so much that we can encourage one or the other to work for God even in unusual ways?

G Prayer

Pray for teamwork of women and men together in serving God and working for good in our world.

H Link work this week

Do what Deborah did. Persuade someone who is apprehensive to do a task they see needs doing. Be prepared to help them.

Study Five

The parents of Samson

Aim: to examine the way God related to the parents of Samson.

A Exploring your experience

1. Have you ever felt tantalised, even annoyed, when somebody else received the information on something that affected you too, and you wanted to be told first hand?

B Life and Times

Judges ruled Israel after Deborah with varying degrees of honesty and of success – Gideon, Tola, Jair, Jephthah. In between times the people of Israel drifted – disorganised and turning often to other gods. When they did this, God allowed them to be harassed or conquered by their enemies. The judges who came out as national heroes did so because they fought their oppressors and regained for Israel their national pride. Samson would be such a judge.

C Biblical Reflection
Judges 13:1-25

2. With whom did the angel of the Lord first make contact? (Note: The 'angel of the Lord' is commonly considered to be an appearance of God.)

3. Though Manoah asked for the angel of the Lord to come again, to whom did the angel appear the second time?

4. What joint effort did the couple make for the angel?

5. Who first recognised the being as the angel of the Lord?

6. Manoah and his wife were scared, but who worked out practically, that they could expect to live?

D Analysis

7. What might be the reasons the angel appeared to the wife? Was this what Manoah expected?

8. Many Christians believe the man must always be head of the family in the sense of authority, but the angel appeared twice to the wife before talking to Manoah and laid on her the accountability for obeying instructions in the family. He gave the instructions to Manoah only in an abbreviated form. What might we learn from the Lord God choosing in this case to deal primarily with the wife and allowing her to relay to Manoah the messages affecting the running of the family?

9. Do you think God worked in this case with a theory of male 'headship'? If God does not always practise the 'headship' of men, is there any reason why we should?

10. Since men and women must give an account to God for their actions (see Romans 14:10, mentioned in Study Two, that we must all stand before the judgment seat of God), what is the weakness of the headship theory?

E Commitment to action

11. How can husbands and wives together obey God, without making decisions that undermine the other's responsibility?

12. How can we encourage women to confidently relate to God without treating their husband as a go-between?

13. In 1 Timothy 2:5 we learn there is only one mediator between God and humans. How can husbands avoid acting as a mediator between their wife and God?

F Questions for couples

14. How would we each have reacted in the circumstances of Manoah and his wife?

15. Do we each listen to the Lord for guidance? And talk over what we are learning as this couple did?

16. What can we learn from this study?

G Prayer

Teach us, Lord and Saviour, to learn each from you in our family life without getting second-hand instructions.

H Link work this week

Explain to a friend what you learnt from this study and why you want to remember it.

Study Six

Abigail and Nabal

Aim: to study the efforts of a woman who did what was right, and how God viewed this.

A Exploring your experience

1. Have you ever thought your partner was making a major mistake and had trouble getting him or her to think again?

B Life and Times

At this stage David was a guerilla chief with a band of men roving the hills of Judea. They were hiding from Saul but made themselves reasonably popular with the people around by protecting their crops and flocks from brigands and rustlers. The hill people's grain crops were probably small with some vineyards and fig trees. Their main livelihood came as graziers or ranchers pasturing sheep and goats over a large area. David's protection of the animals probably saved Nabal many shekels.

C Biblical Reflection
1 Samuel 25

2. What can we learn about the economic position of Nabal and Abigail relative to livestock and servants? v. 2, 42

3. How were Abigail and Nabal each regarded by others? What may have been Abigail's occupation which caused people to think she was clever?

4. When David asked for his men to come to the shearers' feast, was it a fair request or was he picking a quarrel?

5. Describe the steps that escalated the quarrel between David and Nabal. Was the quarrel necessary?

6. When Abigail decided to act in a way that was untraditional for a woman, what impression do you gain of her resourcefulness and efficiency? What did she say to David? What catastrophe did she prevent by her quick action?

7. She both went against her husband and persuaded a guerilla chief not to fight. Which people gained from her action? In what way did Abigail do Nabal a favour? In what way did she do David a favour? v. 26, 33

8. Describe the way David treated Abigail in response to her gift.

9. After Nabal died, presumably with stroke or heart attack, what did David comment on God's judgment of the story?

D Analysis

10. In what circumstances might it be right for a woman to go against her husband? Who should decide when that point is reached?

11. Abigail took an initiative outside her own family and private life, and was praised for it, seemingly with God's approval. How might this effect our thinking about husbands and wives today?

12. A woman, by her diplomacy, saved the lives of all her family's servants and kept David and his men from the guilt of bloodshed. Is diplomacy a skill of many women? When might it be good for a couple to use the wife's diplomatic skills?

13. If God approved Abigail's action, where does this place the 'headship theory' that husbands must always make the rules?

14. A contrast to note. In Acts 5:1-11 Sapphira did not act contrary to her husband. If God wanted women only ever to follow their husband's lead, it was most unfair to strike Sapphira for obeying her husband. But in fact she died for her sin. What does this say about God treating women as responsible for their own actions and therefore not able to leave all decision making to their husbands?

E *Commitment to action*

15. What does this story mean for us today in our families, our churches?

16. Does this story speak about women in the secular structures of our own society? Peacemakers are an important asset in a society. How might we value peacemakers more?

F *Questions for couples*

17. What would I do if you were like Nabal?

18. What would I do if you were like Abigail?

19. How could we work on our peacemaking skills?

G *Prayer*

Pray that both women and men will be strong enough to do right. Pray that all who work for peace in our society will be as successful as Abigail.

H *Link work this week*

Act as a peacemaker in a situation you know of.

Study Seven

The Shunammite couple

Aim: to explore the relationship of a husband and wife team who trusted each other.

A Exploring your experience

1. Think of an occasion in your life when you wished you had more room for hospitality, or were grateful for hospitality received. Describe how you felt.

2. Have you ever been desperately worried for the health of your child?

B Life and Times

In a subsistence society like that of Israel under the kings, there are few hotels and it is thought a common human virtue to shelter travellers. It is still like that today in the hills of a country like Nepal. But it is not normal to build a room for a particular traveller.

It is also common for children to die in societies where people depend only on the resources they can grow. In rural areas of Third World countries still in some parts four in ten children die before age 5 years.

C *Biblical Reflection*
2 Kings 4:8-37

3. Which people in the story make initiatives and suggestions?

4. The woman was not ambitious for herself v.13, yet what can you guess about the economic status of the Shunammite couple?

5. What seems to be the level of communication between the Shunammite husband and wife? How much do they trust each other?

D *Analysis*

6. Elisha and Gehazi seemed to converse readily with the woman rather than the man in a healthy and warm relationship. Did this seem to be a satisfactory way of working from the point of view of all four people?

7. What was the advantage in this story of the level of the husband and wife's trust in each other when a decision had to be made? And if it had to be made in a hurry?

8. Think again of the commonly heard 'headship' theory requiring husbands to take complete authority in a family. Do you think the Shunammite couple practised this? Did anyone expect them to? Did God ask them to?

9. The wife took initiatives in 4:8&10, was humble in 4:13, decisive in 4:22-25, assertive in 4:27-30, and grateful in 4:37. Which of these characteristics would be good for Christian women to model themselves on? Would this make any difference to how husbands and wives relate?

E *Commitment to action*

10. What can we do to encourage adequate models of Christian husbands and wives in
   (a) levels of communication

(b) levels of trust
(c) individual initiatives?

11. What can we do to enable better health care for children in Third World countries today?

F Questions for couples

12. How do we rate in hospitality to God's people or to people who need help?

13. Who takes which initatives with us? Is this how we want it?

14. What do we think about the 'headship theory?' (More on this next study)

G Prayer

Pray for wives and husbands to take initiatives, be humble, decisive, assertive or grateful where these at different times are appropriate God-given virtues.

H Link work this week

Take a hospitality initiative you have often wished you would get around to.

Study Eight

Huldah and Shallum

Aim: to examine the gifts God gave to a woman who used them well for the good of the nation, and the relationship between the woman and her husband over her gifts.

A Exploring your experience

1. Has it ever happened that a man senior to you asked you or a woman you know for advice because of some specialist knowledge? Do the men of your church ask a woman for advice on matters of policy?

B Life and Times

During the reign of the good King Josiah, Hilkiah the high priest had found the book of the law in the house of the Lord and got Shaphan to read it aloud to the king. He was deeply distressed because he realised he and his ancestors had not obeyed the words of the book. He wanted his top advisors to find out from God what he had to do, so they went to the prophetess, the person who was God's representative to his people on earth.

There is no comment that it was unusual for the prophet to be a woman. We find in 2 Kings 23:2 that there were other prophets (people who spoke from God to humans) and priests (people who spoke from the human side to God).

Huldah's message was a stern warning of judgement, but Josiah would live to a peaceable end because he had repented. Josiah was not, however, content to let his people perish. He made all the priests, prophets and people listen to the book of the covenant and watch the king make a covenant to follow the Lord and keep his commandments.

C Biblical Reflection
2 Kings 22:14-20, 2 Chron. 34:14–33

2. How are the following people described in the story?
   a. Hilkiah, b. Shaphan, c. Ahikam, d. Abdon,
   e. Asaiah, f. Huldah, g. Shallum

3. A thought. If Shallum's grandfather was still alive, what age group might Huldah and Shallum be?

4. Most women were illiterate, as was the king apparently. Which of the men would have been literate?

5. Five men in authority, acting for a sixth, a king, went to a young, probably illiterate woman, Huldah, to hear God's voice. What must have gone before to make this a likely scenario?

D Analysis

6. What might have been Shallum's perception of Huldah and his opinion of her ministry and gifts? Do you think he had encouraged her gifts?

7. Think about Huldah's relationship to Shallum. Is there an indication that she related to the rest of the world through her husband, or did she relate in her own right?

8. Did Huldah relate directly to God or through her husband? Some preachers say a husband is a 'covering' for a woman. Is there an indication that Shallum was a 'covering' for Huldah? Is

there any part of the Bible that says a husband must be a 'covering' for a wife?

9. For what reasons did the five men and king Josiah accept Huldah's prophecy?

10. A prophet, speaking the message of God to the people, must be regarded as a person of authority. Are there women in your church who speak the message of God? Are they viewed as people of authority?

E *Commitment to action*

11. What can we do to enable both men and women to respect and encourage the use of each other's gifts, without worrying whether the gift is culturally perceived as feminine or masculine?

12. In the Old Testament prophets spoke out and worked against the wrongs that were in their society. What can we do in our churches to give value to the prophetic work of women and men?

F *Questions for couples*

13. What gifts and abilities do we see in each other?

14. Which of these abilities are spiritual and which practical? Or is there a difference?

15. How can we use these abilities for other people and for God?

16. How can we each encourage the other to use the gifts they have been given?

G *Prayer*

May we recognise all the God-given gifts of husbands and wives and encourage and enable each to use their skills in the widest way.

H Link work this week

For a man: Ask a woman's advice on a matter of policy which she knows something about. For a woman: Ask a younger or quieter woman's advice on something about which she is well informed.

Later: Did you follow the advice?

Study Nine

Elizabeth and Zechariah

Aim: to show how Elizabeth and Zechariah lived with mutual consideration and forgiveness and each had the privilege of speaking the oracles of God.

A Exploring your experience

1. Have you ever been close to someone who has had a deep disappointment in life, or who has a physical disability? How has this made life different for them?

2. Have you ever experienced the power of forgiving to maintain or heal a relationship?

B Life and Times

A barren woman was despised in ancient Jewish society. Women in Elizabeth's circumstances often felt very ashamed, like Hannah in 1 Samuel 1. Yet Elizabeth does not appear to feel like this.

Zechariah probably had only one turn in his life time to burn the incense and make the sacrifice alone in the holiest place. The ritual is described in Leviticus 16:12-19.

C Biblical Reflection
Luke 1:5–25, 39–45, 56–80

3. Zechariah and Elizabeth were both regarded as people of significance in their ability to serve God because of their lineage. v. 5 How were they both regarded in verses 6 and 7? What can you gather of their relationship to each other in verses 5–25?

4. When Elizabeth felt John's movement in response to Mary's message, it was an amazing sign. Perhaps she was spiritually sensitive to recognise it. Then she prophesied loudly. Do you think she was surprised? Did she do it voluntarily? Would she feel she was the instrument of God in doing so?

5. Why might God have given this power to prophesy to Elizabeth rather than Zechariah?

6. There is no indication of Elizabeth and Zechariah were annoyed with each other at any stage, though they could have had reason to be. She was barren for years. He had got into trouble with God for disbelieving the angel. Elizabeth had a spiritual gift, which presumably Zechariah did not have at that stage. What do you think they knew and practised about understanding each other? Do you think they lived with forgiveness to each other?

7. How might Zechariah and Elizabeth have each helped the other during the period of her pregnancy?

8. How did Zechariah and Elizabeth jointly offer haven for the coming Christ? Perhaps their household was talked about among the other priestly families when they sheltered Mary, an unmarried pregnant young woman. How do you think they treated her?

9. Suggest some of the conversation that would have occurred at the rejoicing in verse 57.

D Analysis

10. What about physical disability? How does it affect a marriage?

11. What might have gone before in mutual respect and understanding between Elizabeth and Zechariah to allow for the decision on the child's name in verses 59–63?

12. Who was looking after the affairs of the family during John's circumcision and naming ceremony? Did this seem to be okay? Why would God allow a woman to take the lead at such a crucial time?

13. What was significant about Zechariah's power of speech returning?

14. In verse 67 Zechariah was filled with the Holy Spirit and prophesied. Now the parents had both received this power of God. What might they have said to each other later? How would this affect their mutual respect for each other?

E Commitment to action

15. How can we support couples when a person has a physical disability?

16. How can we encourage a wife or husband to use their spiritual gifts, such as Elizabeth's gift of prophecy, even if their partner is not at the same stage?

F Questions for couples

17. How readily would we shelter a needy person?

18. How well do we get on at practising forgiveness when we feel the other has made a mistake?

19. Have we communicated enough to be able to speak for each other?

20. In this story was it the right thing for one person to move ahead of the other in a spiritual gift? How might it have strengthened them when they both had the gift of prophecy? What would we prefer?

G Prayer

Elizabeth and Zechariah were your aunt and uncle, Jesus, and John's parents. They were your role models as you grew. May we as parents be models of mutual consideration, forgiveness and encouragement. And when you want us to, let either of us speak with your power on us.

H Link work this week

Practise using a gift God gave you.

Study Ten

Mary and Joseph

Aim: to show how God, through Gabriel, put an enormous responsibility on Mary and how Joseph and Mary learnt to trust each other and God's choice.

A Exploring your experience

1. Have you ever experienced a circumstance where you were afraid people would not believe you? Who did believe and trust you?

B Life and Times

The Jews were looking for a Messiah, someone to save them from the Roman domination. But they expected a brilliant leader, a general perhaps, or a king.

People of the time considered a young woman was in her father's care to make decisions for her until she married and then in her husband's care, rather as if she was legally a child all her life. Western society and most others have had the same view for centuries.

C Biblical Reflection
Luke 1:26–56, Matthew 1:18–25, Luke 2:1–7

2. How much do we know, or can we guess, of Mary's circumstances when the angel spoke to her? What might have gone before which made her qualify for this special task?

3. God was commissioning Mary for a task which was perhaps the greatest task God ever asked of a human – to be the mother of the Son of God. How did she respond?

4. When God commissioned Moses, Exodus 3, Gideon, Judges 6, Jeremiah, Jeremiah 1 they tried to say He should not choose them. What made Mary different?

5. Imagine what Mary would feel telling her parents and her fiancé that she was pregnant. How was she spared some of the embarrassment in front of the neighbours?

6. Normally a young woman could not read or write, but what can we discover of Mary's knowledge of the Old Testament when we read the great poetry of verses 46–55? An illiterate village girl would be unlikely to speak such poetry. It may have been a God-given prophecy, or perhaps Mary was literate, soaked in the knowledge of the Old Testament so the words came to her lips.

And then someone wrote down the song of praise, Mary herself, or Zechariah perhaps – or else they sang it often enough to remember it. At least when Luke was collecting the material to write this gospel it was available. Perhaps Mary was a very unusual young woman who had learnt to read, who studied the Old Testament and loved it and the God she read about.

7. Matthew tells how Joseph was not sure about whether to believe Mary. He needed his own visit from an angel. Most of us would not blame him. Do you think Mary and Joseph's trust in each other grew?

8. Mary went on a trip. Who decided this? Did she ask her father or Joseph's permission? This is surprising. Perhaps she took

someone with her for safety as it would take three days walking to reach Elizabeth and Zechariah's place.

D Analysis

9. If decisions concerning women were usually the responsibility of fathers or husbands, why did God not send Gabriel to Mary's father or to Joseph to ask permission for this major dislocation to and apparent disgrace to their family? Was God expecting Mary to make a decision about this in her own right? If so, why?

10. God asked a young woman to agree to a plan that meant she decided something-hugely significant to God's plan for the world-where and among which people the Son of God would appear in the world of humans. What does this say about a woman's responsibilities?

11. Perhaps Joseph too was rather special. Do you think many men in his time would have willingly married a young woman who could read, who had strange things happening in her life that he did not control, who was pregnant yet claimed she was still a virgin, who even went off on a journey down country on her own initiative? What can we respect in him?

12. Mary's first commitment was to obeying God in heaven, not to obeying her father or husband. Is this what we want in Christian marriages today?

E Commitment to action

13. Joseph too must have put the will of God above his personal social comfort. In what ways might this be a model for us today? Are there people or situations God might call us as men or women to associate with in spite of what people think?

14. We have seen a couple supporting each other in very difficult circumstances. How might this change things for marriages we know? How can we support such couples?

15. Mary must have been a thinker in her own right, not leaving all the theorising to Joseph. Luke 2:19 indicates she thought and analysed seriously what had happened. What can we learn from this?

16. How can we plan for both wives and husbands to act as people accountable to God?

F Questions for couples

17. How far are we from the old model of husbands and fathers always making the rules and carrying out the important tasks with a wife's support. Are we nearer to the model that God planned for Joseph and Mary where she had a task to do which he could not do but in which he could support her?

18. How will we raise our sons and daughters to see future husbands and wives as partners and as equals in a team in planning, deciding and working?

G Prayer

Thank you, Saviour in Heaven, for the picture of Joseph who supported his wife through a difficult task, and of Mary who obeyed your call on her life. May we learn from their lives.

Women, Abuse and the Bible

Abuse within the church and home is on the increase, especially among those who hold conservative religious beliefs. This book argues that much of the problem lies with the misuse and misunderstanding of the Bible's teaching on headship and submission.

The contributors, who include counsellors, biblical scholars, an abuser and survivors, draw on recent studies and personal experiences to highlight the issues of domestic, verbal and clergy violence, emotional cruelty, sexual harassment, and rape. They show clearly how the Bible can be used to hurt or to heal, to disperse God's grace or to obstruct it. The final chapters offer a positive theology for the healthy family and a brief epilogue on what churches can do.

This is a valuable resource book for church leaders, counsellors and those who have suffered abuse within the church.

Contributors are Carolyn Holderread Heggen, David M. Scholer, Diane Langberg, Jackie J. Hudson, Alice P. Matthews, Shirley Gillett, Craig S. Keener, M. Gay Hubbard, Joan Burgess Winfrey, Mary Nella Bruce and Steven R. Fleming.

Catherine Clark Kroeger is Adjunct Professor of Classical and Ministry Studies at Gordon-Conwell Theological Seminary.

James R. Beck is Professor of Counselling at Denver Seminary.

Paternoster Press ISBN 0-85364-868-9

paternoster

Domestic Violence and the Church

A thought-provoking look at the true nature of domestic violence including emotional, verbal, economic and physical abuse.

Domestic violence is not just a private family concern, but is a 'public' phenomenon embedded in the structure of our society. Therefore the church's role should not be merely to assist victims caught in violent families but more importantly to help to eradicate domestic violence from our society.

Information about the protection and services available to victims is given together with suggestions as to how the church can assist individual victims.

"Solidarity with the broken-hearted means moving out of our comfort zones. [This book] should be required reading for church leaders, counsellors, and those involved as lay-people in pastoral care."
Roy McCloughry, Director of Kingdom Trust.

"The Church is being increasingly perplexed by domestic situations which in one way or another are related to abuse . . . The writer examines the problem with a sensitive and impartial Christian lawyer's perspective, compassion and expertise."
Eldin R. Corsie, Minister, Christian Life Centre, St Helens.

As a solicitor, Helen Conway specialises in all aspects of Family Law and is involved with the Liverpool and Knowsley Domestic Violence Forums. She has also written *Domestic Violence: Picking up the Pieces* (Lion) a self-help book for victims of domestic violence.

Paternoster Press ISBN 0-85364-817-4

paternoster

When Love Prevails

"When I found Christ, I found a treasure."

Born and raised as a Sikh in India, Narindar felt a sense of evil pursuing her during her early life. Through an arranged marriage she came to Britain. It was there that she came face to face with Christ.

This book tells of Narindar's upbringing and conversion, her struggle with disabling illness and of the work she and her husband began with Asian peoples in Britain. Through all the joys, fears and frustrations, Narindar discovered that 'when love prevails' there is no stopping God or his Holy Spirit from working.

"Narindar and Margaret are living testimonies of God's love and grace working powerfully in, and through, his children . . . There are not many books or resources to help with outreach to the Sikh community. This book is a very timely addition."
Ram Gidoomal, Chairman of South Asian Concern

"This book tells the remarkable story of a Sikh couple's journey to faith in Christ. For those who are born and brought up in a Christian family and a Christian environment, Christ and Christianity, whilst very meaningful, may not always have such sharp definition and clarity. Narindar Mehat's testimony gives these sharp contrasts, like the light of the morning sun shattering the surrounding darkness . . . A very personal book and a very valuable one."
Dr Patrick Sookdeo, Director of the Barnabas Fund

"An interesting testimony of how an Asian couple came to commit their lives to Christ. This commitment has been costly for them, not least in responding to God's call."
The Right Rev. Dr. Michael Nazir-Ali, Bishop of Rochester

Narindar Mehat and her husband, Sewa work among Asians in Wolverhampton with Beracah Christian Ministries.

OM Publishing ISBN 1-85078-288-1

OM
publishing